It Takes Two

Gene Boccialetti

It Takes Two

Managing Yourself
When Working with Bosses
and Other Authority Figures

Jossey-Bass Publishers • San Francisco

Quote used as epigraph in the preface from THE PRACTICE OF MANAGEMENT by PETER F. DRUCKER. Copyright 1954 by Peter F. Drucker. Copyright renewed © 1982 by Peter F. Drucker. Preface copyright © 1986 by Peter F. Drucker. Reprinted by permission of HarperCollins Publishers, Inc.

Substantial discounts on bulk quantities of Jossey-Bass books are available to corporations, professional associations, and other organizations. For details and discount information, contact the special sales department at Jossey-Bass Inc., Publishers. (415) 433–1740; Fax (800) 605–2665.

For sales outside the United States, please contact your local Paramount Publishing International Office.

TCF Manufactured in the United States of America on Lyons Falls Pathfinder Tradebook. This paper is acid-free and 100 percent totally chlorine-free.

Library of Congress Cataloging-in-Publication Data

Boccialetti, Gene.
    It takes two : managing yourself when working with bosses and other authority figures / Gene Boccialetti. — 1st ed.
        p.   cm. — (The Jossey-Bass management series)
    Includes bibliographical references (p.   ) and index.
    ISBN 0-7879-0088-5
    1. Managing your boss.   2. Interpersonal relations.   I. Title.
II. Series.
HF5548.83.B63   1995
650.1'3—dc20   95-6442

FIRST EDITION
HB Printing   10 9 8 7 6 5 4 3 2 1

The Jossey-Bass Management Series

To my teachers,
especially Robert E. Kaplan
and Donald M. Wolfe

Contents

Preface

> I have yet to sit down with a manager, whatever his
> level of job, who was not primarily concerned with
> his upward relations and upward communications.
> — *Peter Drucker*

It Takes Two is about how managers at all organizational levels work with (or in opposition to) their bosses, their managers, their leadership. It is a book that talks about both effective and ineffective ways of managing the relationship with your bosses and other people in positions of organizational authority.

Managing this relationship has always been important because of its effects on your ability to do your job, your access to resources and information, your job satisfaction, performance evaluations, and career progress. This relationship also affects the ethical context for managerial behavior. This is something that has been much discussed recently as the behavior of managers under the direction of their bosses and others in organizational authority has also come under scrutiny.

But even though this upward relationship has always been important to managers, it has become even more so because of all the changes that are occurring in organizations. There are many changes happening in the ways we organize, lead, and manage modern enterprises. Many if not most of them involve a fundamental rethinking and renegotiation of the way people at all levels manage their relationship with people in authority.

Current Trends in Managing and Leading

We have been hearing a lot lately about many kinds of changes taking place in organizations, particularly leadership and design changes, and the other important corollary changes such as empowerment, reengineering, total quality management, and greater use of self-managed teams and strategic business units. We are changing roles and relationships throughout organizations and trying to provide more of a voice in decision making to people at all levels.

This is not just a management fad, although, regrettably, many are approaching it as if it were. Global demands for adaptability, flexibility, lower costs, and higher quality make such changes a make-or-break necessity. Such demands are not likely to disappear; we are witnessing massive and historic changes to governments and economies around the world. The ability to respond to more localized contingencies and produce high-quality products and services in a timely and efficient manner requires that we push resources, discretion, and responsibility further down in our organizational structures. Organizations that hope to survive and prosper in the new emerging world order will heed this call and make such changes permanent, a new way of thinking and a new way of life.

And while we are changing our approach to leading and managing, we are also asking that others begin to change how they relate to those in higher levels of authority. It is not an overstatement to argue that we are fundamentally rewiring our conceptions of management and the premises for the managerial relationship, in both directions.

It is tempting, when we discuss upward relationships, to confine our thinking to those at the lowest operating levels of organizations. However, it is both true and important to note that such relationships are an important part of everyone's work life. Virtually everyone has a boss (sometimes several) and everyone has to manage himself or herself in this relationship. But, strangely, it is less acknowledged, as we address the changes managers should be making in their approach to leading—the "downward" view—that there are many changes they must also make in their authority relationships—the "upward" view—as well.

To look at training and educational curricula, textbooks, training materials, and the like, the need to change the management of our relationships to authority is infrequently recognized or not recognized at all. It is the more amazing when we recognize that the changes mentioned above represent a massive upheaval that is calling upon managers at all levels of organization to alter the fundamental premises that have guided their relationships to organizational authority for decades.

In this relationship, we are now beginning to emerge from the dominant military metaphor that has implicitly guided our thinking and behavior for a very long time. Gone are the days when managers were best advised to be the "good soldier," when obedience to authority was a primary virtue and uncritical and uncomplaining implementation of directives would gain the manager security and promotions. The role and the management of authority relationships have become much more complex. It is ironic that though we call it the military metaphor, there is much data, as recent as the war in the Persian Gulf, that suggests the military itself has taken significant steps to move away from this tired conception of relating to authority.

Though "good soldiering" and skills at efficient implementation will continue to have a place in organizations, they are not enough any longer to guarantee managers ongoing security or advancement. Concerns about flexibility, versatility, and added value now suggest that managers must learn other ways of operating in their relationships to their bosses and others in organizational authority.

More and more, organizational leaders are coming to expect from their managers greater initiative and less passivity; more risk taking and less risk avoidance; more commitment and less accommodation; being informed about the issues and pushing for influence instead of "yessing" people to death; pursuing ongoing development, training for flexibility, and creating multiple skill sets; understanding and aligning themselves with larger organizational purposes and goals and accepting personal responsibility instead of protesting "I was just doing what I was told." Pursuing opportunity instead of pursuing security may well become the hallmark for the successful manager.

But even as these changes occur and we hear more about autonomy and discretion, self-managing and so on, we must realize that there continues to be an ongoing and important role for authority in organizations. Though often ineptly handled, authority performs too many vital functions, particularly in large-scale systems, for us to leave it in the dustbin. Overall needs for information channeling and coordination of effort, particularly in large-scale systems, demand the continuing use of authority in some form.

I am reminded of the experience of Allan Kennedy, coauthor with Terrence Deal of the popular book *Corporate Cultures* (1982), and the lessons he learned on this issue. When Kennedy tried to create a company using the precepts advanced in his book, he discovered, with much pain, the importance of strong centralized authority, direction, accountability, and discipline. His frequent absences and excessive staff autonomy in his Boston company, Selkirk, led to confusion, lowered performance, strained friendships, and interdepartmental strife. In one month, while the company was losing money, three of his four salespeople decided to take vacations at the same time. Sales for that month "all but vanished." Kennedy joked, somewhat ruefully, about naming his next book *Kicking Ass and Taking Names* (Rhodes, 1990, pp. 300, 302).

Situational Followership

As is the case with approaches to leadership that suggest situational awareness and adaptability, we must learn how and when to adapt our subordinate style to the various situations that we face in our work with our bosses and others in organizational authority. No one approach is going to suit all the varied situations we face. Sometimes, as in a crisis, we will need skills at timely and efficient execution of directives. But at other times, perhaps when we are facing complex and unstructured problems where no one has the decisive expertise and we must move in concert with other functions, we will need to push for influence and assert ourselves in the decision-making process with our bosses.

What all this adds up to is a role that has become much more complex, demanding, difficult, and confusing. Like the contingency or situational thinking that has come to dominate leadership practice, managers are being called upon to adapt themselves in the authority relationship as well.

Style Groove

In my research that provided the basis for this book, I learned that managers have a style, or a preferred approach and reflexive set of behaviors, that they use in managing themselves in the relationship to authority. While managers make surface accommodations to any particular boss, there is an underlying stratum of values, attitudes, and convictions that forms a more enduring approach to their boss-subordinate relationships. In fact, I learned about nine common styles that managers use in their relationship with their bosses.

In addition to the existence of styles, I learned that managers are usually unaware of their style, and because of that style, they differ dramatically in their receptivity to the organizational changes proposed or under way in our organizations. Particularly where managers have established, due to personal leanings and decades of organizational socialization, a preference for accommodating organizational authority, they tend not to be very receptive to many new-age enticements such as empowerment and participation in decision making. It is worth noting that, in my research, the accommodating styles account for over half of the participating managers in business organizations.

I also learned that these styles, while changeable with some guidance and concerted effort, tend not to change. A major culprit in this inertia is the failure of organizations to systematically address this issue and the widespread difficulties managers have (along with their bosses) in discussing the functioning of their relationship.

Even as managers are being encouraged (or told) to change the way they lead and manage, there has been no way for them to assess their subordinate style. There has been little or no guidance about what directions to go in changing their subordinate styles, and there has been little or no guidance about how to do it. How, in this new organizational order, should they manage themselves in their upward relationships?

It is a bit like a journey in unfamiliar terrain. First, you need to know where you are. Second, you need to know which direction to move toward. And third, you need support to get from point A to point B.

This is what *It Takes Two* is about.

Some Common Fallacies

It Takes Two will also contradict several fallacies about this important relationship.

The first fallacy I have already hinted at: the belief that the leadership relationship (the "looking down" view) is the only really important thing to address and to change. Managers themselves consistently report how critical the relationship is with their bosses, how managing upward is a crucial skill. And, as we attempt leadership change, we must remember that we cannot change a relationship by addressing only one party to that relationship, the higher-power one. If we want leadership change, we will also have to address those who are on the receiving end of these new visions of organizational leadership.

The second fallacy is that managers *know* how to adapt their style to these proposed changes. There is little to support this idea in management textbooks and organizational training curriculum. It is a topic that is rarely, if ever, addressed. Until now, there have been no ways for managers to perform theory-guided and validated self-assessment. And because of confusing organizational signals, most managers are quite uncertain about how their organizations want them to act. Some organizations seem to be susceptible to management fashion and fads and appear, over the long term, to be unwilling to make the basic changes necessary to truly empower people at all levels. For these managers, in particular, flexibility will be quite important in this relationship.

All managers have a subordinate style, a pattern of behavior in how they approach their relationships with their bosses. While many find this idea novel, I will present nine common subordinate styles among managers and show how, or whether, these styles lend themselves to many of the current changes taking place in organizations.

The third fallacy among managers is that managing your boss is the thing to do. This approach to the relationship denies important reality, a fact of organizational life, and the responsibility of managers for those who report to them. The manipulative encouragements and salacious gossip often found in this popular literature tend to encourage continued game playing in a relationship that must, in order to be effective, be placed on a solid footing of trust and authenticity. Attempts to manage the boss threaten to turn the relationship agenda into one where equalization of power, nonauthentic behavior, information suppression, and playing games become a preoccupation. A better strategy is to learn how to manage *yourself* in the relationship with your boss. We can no longer do without the relationship synergies that are possible when critical organizational partners work together.

The fourth fallacy is that managers who get along well with their bosses have little to gain by examining their conduct in this relationship. One thing I have realized through this work is that you can feel that you are a master at managing your relationship with your boss and at the same time be colluding in creating ineffective relationships. Effectiveness, not comfort, should be your goal. A boss and a subordinate can create a relationship that is pleasant and agreeable *and* be wholly ineffective at their task (or parts of it). What this means is that in any relationship with authority, in order to be effective, sometimes both of you will need to be uncomfortable.

I will also show you that many managers make substantial errors in their guesstimates of the relationship quality with their bosses. They are often shocked and angered to discover the boss's reality about their relationship does not reflect their own understanding. This attribution error has had some tragic consequences for performance appraisals, promotional opportunities, and, in the case of downsizings, even job retention. In the rash of wrongful-dismissal lawsuits filed in recent years, a common culprit has been the failure of managers (both bosses and subordinates) to validate and communicate their views of their relationship as well as the subordinate managers' performance.

The fifth fallacy is that there is a single best way to manage this relationship and that managers can figure it out without assistance. For work effectiveness and for management development (which supports long-term effectiveness), managers need to be versatile and flexible and adapt their approach in this relationship to the tasks they and their bosses face. And they need guidance and support in order to do it. General advice that exacts a promise to do better in the future is not likely to yield much change. *It Takes Two* provides specific advice and guidance, not only about your default style in managing this relationship but also about how to adapt it to address the range of tasks you face with your bosses.

The research process that forms the basis for this book spanned the years from 1983 to 1994. During that time, I met, spoke with, and interviewed hundreds of managers and executives from business organizations, health care, government, education, military, and social service organizations, representing virtually all the common organizational functions (marketing, sales, manufacturing, human resources, engineering, research and development, quality control, management, information systems, and finance and accounting). In addition, more than eleven hundred participants completed a research questionnaire that reflected their views about this relationship. In the final analysis, I used some 630 of these managers' scores and score patterns on the self-assessment inventory and research questionnaire to refine the concepts and profiles presented in this book. (For more details on the research and analysis processes, you may refer to the Appendixes at the back of the book.)

Who the Book Is For

This book is addressed to all those, no matter what their level, who have an upward-reporting relationship to someone else or are, even occasionally, accountable to higher-level authority. I suppose the book is intended, for that matter, for all those who have ever wondered about how they handle themselves with people in authority, whether they feel they have been largely successful or not.

Although I frequently refer to managers and those in staff positions in business organizations, it does not matter whether you are in business or not. Many of the people who told me about their issues and experiences are from business. But many are from health care, social service and mental health organizations, educational institutions, the military, and government organizations.

How the Book Can Be Useful

I often say that maps and compasses are of little use if you do not know where you are.

In managing yourself in the relationship to organizational authority, this book will make a case for a new perspective or theory of this relationship that does not rely on traditional theories. It is a view that is largely suggested by managers and staff participants and it is *for* managers (and those at all levels who have to deal with someone in authority). It is a new map of the relationship terrain between you and the people in authority you deal with.

You will see that in your approach, suggested by self-diagnostic questions at the start of Chapters Two, Three, and Four, certain elements are useful and effective at some times and in some situations. In the history that managers have enjoyed, stability of career paths and organizational environments have permitted these relatively unvarying approaches to work. But with all the changes being pushed on us, we now need to learn to round out our flat sides, develop additional skills, to be flexible, to consciously choose and adapt our subordinate style.

And, through providing opportunity for self-assessment, this book can help you to appreciate where you are starting from in addressing these changes. What is your style in managing the relationship with people in authority? How well and under what circumstances does it work? Also, there is no doubt that under other circumstances your style does not work as well. We know for example that one of the primary career derailers is ineffective management of the relationship with one's boss. Managers commonly take approaches that were effective at one organizational level and try to use them when they move to higher levels or to a different organization.

Finally, the book will provide you with a compass that will say, "This way is the direction for you to move in managing yourself with authority." It is a way of pathfinding that is quite synergistic with the current trends in today's organizations, but it also has great value even if your organization continues to function in more traditional ways. I know you will find it useful either way.

Layout of the Book

Chapter One summarizes the new set of ideas, the three dimensions that make up your style. It also shows you how those three dimensions come together in various ways (in varying intensities) to form a particular style. My research with executives and managers found nine basic styles in organizations. In this chapter are the book's largest headlines, the big picture.

Chapters Two, Three, and Four discuss the three elements of style—deference, distance, and divergence—in turn. They sketch out the core issues, advantages, and potential liabilities in each dimension and describe how managers think and act who score high and low on each. At the end of each chapter are decision rules, providing advice about when to do what.

Chapter Five contains more detail on the nine different styles that my research found were the most common combinations of the three elements. When you read this, keep in mind that, in addition to having one of these styles yourself, you probably supervise or work with people who fit into one or another of these styles. There are helpful hints about how to manage yourself as well as how to approach subordinates who are likely to show some of these characteristics.

Chapter Six tells you in some detail how to be more effective in the relationship with your bosses. It discusses how to better manage yourself in the authority relationship and under what circumstances your style works best. Just as important—perhaps even more so—it tells under what circumstances your style is likely to fail you. Here you can figure out how to complement your approach, round out the flat sides.

Chapter Seven is addressed to you as a boss (the rest of the book addresses you as someone with a reporting relationship to someone else). Or, if you like, it is addressed to *your* boss. As you read it, consider how you encourage your subordinates to relate to you. Have your boss read it, then discuss it. If you are smart, you will get some feedback from your boss and give some thought to how you encourage your direct reports to relate to you.

Chapter Eight discusses organizational-level issues. This chapter takes the viewpoint of policy makers and addresses the role that these ideas can have in the context of many of the current change efforts under way in organizations.

Following Chapter Eight are the Appendixes. For those with a more quantitative orientation or research leaning, in this section I discuss method and present some of the statistical foundations for this work as well as the results of smaller related studies that I conducted on authority relations.

Acknowledgments

This has been a long process, one that I started in 1983, and it has involved a lot of people in differing capacities. As with any research process that grounds itself in organizational and managerial reality, I owe the largest debt to the people who discussed their approach to authority in their organizational lives. Many managers and executives thoughtfully shared their understandings and questions with me and often their emotions as well. The students from the Executive M.B.A. program and the Day M.B.A. program at the Whittemore School of Business and Economics were especially helpful. I promised confidentiality to them all so I cannot name them, but it is to them I owe the greatest debt.

I also want to thank my colleagues and friends who supported me, prompted my thinking, shared their views and experience, and provided access to people and data that I would not have normally come into contact with. These friends alerted me to interesting sources and anecdotes. This group of valued colleagues and friends includes Marcy Crary at Bentley College, Jeff Petee at Rockwell Corporation, Bill Van Buskirk at La Salle University, Elliott Carlisle at the University of Massachusetts, Amherst, and Ron Fry and Hank Jonas at Case Western Reserve University.

My thanks also to the Portland contingent, which included Craig Cleaves, Joe Melnick, and the South Street Regulars, who helped me keep my balance during hard times.

As for the researching and the writing of the numerous versions of the manuscript, I also want to thank the graduate assistants over the years who spent many hours on the phone, in dusty library shelves on my behalf, or reading and responding to sections of the manuscript. I particularly want to acknowledge the assistance of Lorraine Thompson, Diane Vidala, and Lynn Morganstern.

For support and encouragement as well as responding to such questions as "Is this readable?" I want to thank a number of my colleagues at the University of New Hampshire. I particularly want to thank Jeff Sohl, my resident statistics consultant, who demonstrated remarkable generosity with his advice and guided me through some critical quantitative passages. Bob Puth, Rita Weathersby, Craig Wood, Allen Kaufman, and Steve Fink read sections of the book and reviews and gave me honest and sensitive feedback. I appreciate their individual and collective willingness to help me protect the most valuable of resources in an endeavor like this: my time.

I am indebted as well to John Freear, the associate dean of the Whittemore School of Business and Economics, for his support and sympathetic ear whenever I needed to bend a rule or two. I was also impressed by and am grateful to the reviewers for Jossey-Bass, who clearly oriented themselves to making the project successful, not merely to finding fault with the manuscript.

My thanks, too, to Carol True, our management department administrator and secretary. Although I word processed this manuscript myself, she provided innumerable supports—from faxes to express packages to finding the right kind of paper for my printer to keeping a balky administration functioning in support of my completing the manuscript. I also want to thank Sinthy Kounlasa for her support in the early years of this work and for helping me not to take myself too seriously.

In the preparation of the final manuscript, I owe a great deal to Bill Drath at the Center for Creative Leadership, whose role as my development editor felt like a gift and a godsend. His repeated insights into me, my expression, and my work truly transformed the final versions of the manuscript and gave me new ways to think about my writing and myself. He and Bill Hicks, my editor at Jossey-Bass, gave me the needed encouragement, gentle challenge, and support to bring my ideas out of the ether and onto the page.

And for Kathy Williams, who in the last two years accepted much less than was her due, while I labored, fumed, and obsessed to complete the job.

Portsmouth, New Hampshire   Gene Boccialetti
March 1995

The Author

Gene Boccialetti is associate professor of organizational behavior at the Whittemore School of Business and Economics at the University of New Hampshire in Durham. He received his B.S. degree (1969) in industrial management from Fairfield University (Fairfield, Connecticut) and his Ph.D. degree (1982) in organizational behavior from the Weatherhead School of Management at Case Western Reserve University.

Before joining the faculty at the University of New Hampshire, Boccialetti worked for several years as an organizational consultant in private practice. During this period, his main client was the Ford Motor Company, where he worked (in numerous sites) on Ford's quality improvement and employee involvement process. Since then, his client organizations have also included the U.S. Air Force, AT&T, Helene Curtis Industries, the Federal Aviation Administration, several major hospitals, and municipal and state government organizations.

In addition to the authority relations research that is the basis of this book, Boccialetti's main research activities have focused on the effectiveness of organizational change efforts and on executive learning and development. He has published articles on the effectiveness of quality improvement efforts, team development, career development, ethics and organizational development, diversity training, and the application of organizational development to community-based human service organizations.

Boccialetti is active with the Academy of Management and the

Organizational Behavior Teaching Society. In addition, he is a certified member of Professional Ski Instructors of America and can be found most weekends during the winter at Loon Mountain in Lincoln, New Hampshire.

It Takes Two

Chapter One

Managing Yourself, Not the Boss: A Look at Your Style

The fault, dear Brutus, is not in our stars,
But in ourselves, that we are underlings.
"Brutus" and "Caesar." What should be in that
"Caesar"?
Why should that name be sounded more than yours?
Write them together: yours is as fair a name.
Sound them: it doth become the mouth as well.
Weigh them: it is as heavy. Conjure with 'em:
"Brutus" will start a spirit as soon as "Caesar."

—Julius Caesar 1.2.134–137

It was a beautiful night on the Chesapeake Bay. Two ships, the Coast Guard cutter *Cuyahoga* and a large cargo ship, the *Santa Cruz II*, were sailing near each other in calm waters.[1] There was no fog. There was no reason for extraordinary caution, nothing to suggest cause for alarm.

The captain of the cutter saw two lights on the cargo ship, indicating to him that it was moving in the same direction as his own ship. The cutter's first mate saw three lights on the cargo ship and determined, without comment, that it was moving *toward* them. The lookout on the cutter also saw the ship, also saw that it was moving toward the cutter, but considered it unnecessary to alert the captain, since he knew that the captain had already taken notice of the cargo ship and its course. The lookout assumed that the captain realized that the cargo ship was moving toward them, not with them.

Over the next few minutes, the Coast Guard captain continued to construct a false view of the situation. Although the two ships were actually approaching each other at full speed, he thought that his own ship was overtaking the second ship very quickly and that the other vessel must therefore be a slow fishing boat. In the final moments as they drew near, based on his presumptions, the captain ordered a turn to port, thinking he would give the presumed fishing boat room to turn. In carrying out this maneuver, the captain placed the cutter directly in the path of a ship four times the cutter's length. The resulting collision killed eleven Coast Guardsmen.

What caused this accident? Was it the captain's error? Many would say it was. After all, leaders are responsible for what happens on their watch, and when they make such an error, we can say they are at fault. But consider this: As the collision neared, the lookout and another seaman discussed the situation. They had seen the cargo ship earlier and knew the captain had seen it as well. They assumed he understood, as they did, that the ship was coming toward them. They evidently figured it would be presumptuous and vaguely insubordinate to alert the captain again.

Even as the captain's actions doomed the ship, his crew, people who knew better, executed his instructions and continued to defer to him and his tragically inverted view of the situation. Their unwillingness, or inability, to step outside their customary relationship with their captain cost many lives. This view of the situation may lead some to say that the fault was with the crew. They should have been more assertive with the captain; they should have questioned his orders.

Rather than trying to locate the cause with either, I think it is more accurate to understand the cause as a systems failure, a failure that includes both the captain and the crew. Commercial airlines have begun to recognize this fact and, through training programs that emphasize team functioning in the cockpit, have encouraged and empowered crew members to be active in problem solving and decision making, even to the point of challenging the captain, and if need be, taking physical control of an aircraft.

Looking at the *Cuyahoga* accident in this larger systems perspective helps us see that even good leaders will make mistakes. To believe otherwise would require an almost childlike view of the role of authority and leadership in organizations. Organizations face many requirements, and their environments are often turbulent and quickly changing. Their functions are too specialized and everyone is spread too thin (particularly as organizations downsize) for anyone (including people in authority) to be on top of everything all the time.

In any effective and healthy organization there must be a tacit, if not explicit, understanding that it is everyone's job to help make others competent and to do what needs to be done to avert serious harm and assure effective outcomes. From this view, those in positions of authority and leadership must be able to rely on those in subordinate positions (which is to say, nearly everyone) to lend their expertise, their perspectives, and their corrective influence and action to decisions.

Only when this occurs will tragic accidents such as that of the *Cuyahoga* be avoided. The tragedy of the *Cuyahoga* is thus more than a failure of leadership and also more than a failure of followers. It is better understood as a failure of the boss-subordinate *relationship*. It was the action of the captain in relation to the action of the subordinates that caused the tragedy. This brings us directly to the issue addressed in this book: how the relationship between bosses and subordinates works and what you, in your role as a subordinate, can do to make the relationship more effective.

Manage Your Boss?

This is not a book about how to manage your boss. It is a book about how to manage *yourself*. More specifically, it is a book about how to manage yourself in the relationship with your boss. Much has been written about styles of leadership. This book is about your style as a subordinate.

While managers have supervisory responsibilities for people who report to them, they also have reporting relationships upward. It is this upward-looking relationship that we are concerned with here: the manager as subordinate. "Good managers recognize that a relationship with a boss involves mutual dependence and that, if it is not managed well, they cannot be effective in their jobs. . . . Effective managers take time and effort to manage not only relationships with their subordinates, but also those with their bosses" (Gabarro and Kotter, 1980, p. 92).

Managers use a wide range of strategies in attempting to deal with their bosses. It is an important relationship and people spend a lot of energy on it. Perhaps because of this, books about managing the boss have become popular. They seem to offer advice on how to make the relationship more effective. Most of these books, however, are little more than collections of pop-psychological myths spiked with numerous manipulative encouragements: how to "one-up" your boss; how to find someone else to deliver bad news to your boss; when communicating with your boss, how to use numbers to convey a cool objectivity.

While the "managing your boss" approach seems to be popular, it results in misdirected efforts because it deflects attention away from the subordinate manager's values, attitudes, and behaviors, and because it perpetuates a stereotype of people in authority. It is an approach that favors managing someone else—the boss—and not the self-as-subordinate. Instead of "How do I handle myself in the relationship?" the question tends to become "How can I maneuver more effectively around my boss, or manipulate him, to get what I want?"

Advice like that in the "managing your boss" literature actually does more to create mistrust and stereotyping in a relationship that has enough problems already. Such advice tends to keep the adversarial tone and manipulative game playing alive, and deflects attention away from the critical issues of boss-subordinate effectiveness.

Why then would such books be popular? Maybe because blaming the boss is easier. It is often a little daunting to pause and consider, for a few moments, the part we ourselves play in a difficult relationship with a boss. Listen, for example, to an executive who is also an M.B.A. student as she reflects on this.

> We had broken up into our groups to discuss the issue. I remember complaining an awful lot about my boss to the others in my group. I must have gone on for about five minutes when Jeff politely interrupted. He said, "Jan, we are not supposed to be discussing what your boss is like, but what you are going to do about improving, or managing that relationship. What about your own behavior?"
>
> Needless to say I was more than a little red in the face. . . . I knew he was right. . . . I left class that day with some feelings of guilt. When it came right down to it, had I really made an effort to communicate my feelings to [my boss]? I had to answer that I hadn't.

Subordinate Style

People at all organizational levels are concerned about the boss-subordinate relationship. Yet learning about themselves in the subordinate role in this relationship is rare. It is a topic that is hardly ever addressed in executive and management training sessions. In earlier career preparation, there is also little discussion of these issues and this relationship. The topic is avoided even though it is quite important in organizational life. As noted career researcher Edgar Schein at M.I.T. has pointed out, "Where his education has taught the graduate principles of how to manage others and to take the corporate point of view, his organizational socialization tries to teach him how to be a good subordinate, how to be influenced, and how to sell ideas from a position of low power" (Schein, 1984, p. 18).

Managers may thus not be getting any introduction in formal training to something they need to know on the job: how to be an effective subordinate. In this book I will suggest that being an effective subordinate starts with identifying your particular subordinate style—that is, with understanding your own way of being a subordinate.

We all approach relationships with people in authority with our own mix of concerns, beliefs, and values. These develop early in life and are modified through education, work, and observing people in positions of authority. Our early and subsequent experience with authority thus sets our basic orientation toward authority. While we will make certain surface adjustments or accommodations to any particular boss, our underlying orientation tends to remain the same from one boss to another. So, regardless of how I might be "forced" to behave with a particular boss, my underlying conviction about what our relationship should be like remains in place.

This underlying orientation is our subordinate style. It can be useful to think of such style as a "grooved" sort of behavior. It is like a reflex that governs our actions and reactions, unless we are consciously choosing to alter our behavior.

The idea of a subordinate style may be novel to you, but consider how frequently we refer to the notion of style in other ways. We refer to style of dress. We talk about a manager's leadership style. Or we refer to more general behavior ("That's not her style"). The idea in this book is that, as with other forms of style, we each have a grooved, accustomed way of thinking and acting when dealing with bosses. This subordinate style, depending on the situation we are in, has a lot to do with how effective we are in these relationships. When our style is wrong for the situation, we will more often than not find ourselves being ineffective.

In the chapters to come, I will have more to say about how to figure out what your style is, when it is likely to work well and not work so well, and how you can adjust it depending on the circumstances you face. Before the end of this chapter I will tell you what I think makes up subordinate style. But first, let us discuss the term, the very idea of being subordinate. Some people are uncomfortable in even thinking of themselves as subordinates, and furthermore the role of subordinate seems to be changing in organizations.

The Changing Subordinate

Bolman and Deal (1984) define authority as all people "who have a legitimate and formal prerogative to make decisions which are binding on others" (p. 113). Virtually all of us in organizations have a reporting relationship that goes upward to someone in authority. Yet this fact does little to explain or counter the negative reaction many of us have to the word *subordinate*. Instead of thinking of the word in terms of legitimate authority structures, we have come to equate the term with subservience.

Listen, for example, to an executive talk about the word.

> Let me begin by saying the word *subordinate* is rather harsh. Webster defines the word in numerous ways: one, placed in, or belonging to a lower order or rank; two, of less importance, secondary; three, subject to or under the authority of a superior; and four, subservient or inferior. It would also be nice if the words *manager* and *superior* were removed from our repertoire of words because of what they connote. "Superiority" and "inferiority" abound with the use of these terms. It is no wonder conflict exists.

Partly because of this kind of discomfort with the word *subordinate* and the concept it implies, we are witnessing attempts in many organizations to find different terms, such as *associate* or *colleague*, to apply to these working relationships. I, too, have struggled to find a less "loaded" way to refer to this relationship. All the terms that I came up with, like those that others have used (*followers, direct reports*), seem somewhat tortured, not entirely accurate, and encumbered with their own baggage. Ultimately I concluded that we have imbued the term *subordinate* with too much power. It simply conveys placement in a hierarchical ordering of relationships; it should not connote anything else, especially not subservience. Even General Colin Powell referred to himself as a "servant" and a "subordinate," and I have never heard anyone accuse him of being subservient.

In some exchanges with people in corporate settings, it began to appear as if many hoped that the hierarchy would itself somehow disappear if we stopped referring to it. However, no matter what words we use to describe them, vertical relationships are unlikely to disappear anytime soon. Even though we have often paid too much attention to vertical layering in organizations and such distinctions have carried too much weight, those relationships will always be necessary in complex organizational systems.

And empowerment, which we have been hearing about for some time now, does not change that. Although empowerment seeks to alter both the approach of leaders and (though not often addressed) the approach to being a subordinate, it does not eliminate vertical relationships. It does suggest that those in so-called subordinate positions will need to behave differently than they may have in the past. As opportunities for autonomy and self-control increase, subordinate managers (that is, all managers) will need to take more initiative, risk, and responsibility. They will need to become proactive in their relationships with authority, argue a point of view, and stay well informed about organizational goals and values. The point is clear: Those who are on the receiving end of empowerment will have their own changes to make.

This book, however, is not only about being empowered. The journey to this kind of change is full of setbacks. Many organizations, for example, when business is bad, renege on good intentions to distribute decision-making power. An article in *Fortune* magazine referred to this as "yo-yo empowerment" (Kiechel, 1992, p. 153). It pointed out that when profit margins decline, so does the room for error, leaving many organizations less willing to experiment with different ways of doing things. The lesson seems to be that managers need to have some degree of flexibility in approaching relationships with authority.

Whether or not these trends continue, whether or not empowerment or self-managed teams or flatter structures appear to be taking root in our organizational landscape, most of us will continue to have a reporting relationship to someone in a position of greater authority. As our organizations change—at whatever speed—we will all need to become more adept at managing this important relationship. To do this, we need to become aware that we have a style and what our particular style is. Then we need to learn how to adjust that style as conditions change.

In short, the rapidly changing demands affecting our organizations require a sort of adaptive competence, a flexibility that allows our organizations to adjust to circumstances. This flexibility depends on flexible relationships with authority. Both leading and creative following skills are necessary; so is the capacity to shift from one set of skills to the other.

In a crisis, when time is of the essence, subordinates will need to be excellent at taking direction and getting the job done. However, when faced with difficult long-term challenges that require creativity, subordinates must be willing and able to stand up and push back to make certain their ideas are heard. Just as we adapt and adjust our approaches to being a boss, we can and should adapt our approach to being a subordinate.

Factors in Subordinate Style

What exactly do I mean by subordinate style? What makes up this kind of grooved behavior we seem to have in relationship to people in authority? My answer to this question is based on research I did with 630 practicing managers between 1983 and 1994. Most of them were from business organizations, but there were also participants from health care, government, education, military, and social service organizations. They represented many different types of organizations and virtually all the common organizational functions: marketing, sales, manufacturing, human resources, engineering, R&D, quality control, management information systems, and finance and accounting. (For more characteristics of the research population, see the Appendixes at the end of the book.)

I identified three main factors that make up subordinate style: deference, distance, and divergence. Each factor arises from a question that managers typically ask themselves in their relationships with their bosses. In effect, if we were to find out your answer to each of these three main questions, we could go a long way toward predicting how you respond to people in authority.

Deference

Deference asks the question: How important is it that I hold onto a large share of power in relationship to my boss and try to exert influence in decision making?

Some managerial subordinates feel that a primary aspect of the subordinate role, at any level, is to push back, resist, counterargue. They want a large say in problem solving and decision making. They tend to be uncomfortable with implementing decisions they did not have a hand in making, particularly where the reasoning behind the decision is unclear to them. They feel the boss should consult with them and listen to their advice. They tend to trust their own judgments and ideas at least as much as they do the boss's. These managers are low in deference.

Other managerial subordinates place much less importance on how much power they have in the relationship with their bosses. These managers are content to let their bosses sort out priorities and solve problems. They may act more as good soldiers and prefer to have their impact through action and implementation. They like the boss to be clear and provide structure and guidance. They tend to give greater consideration to their boss's views and judgment. These managers are high in deference.

Distance

Distance asks the question: How important is it that I establish a person-to-person, not just a role-to-role, relationship with my bosses?

A manager who is oriented to a more personal relationship has a low-distance style. Such a manager believes that a boss and a subordinate should establish more personal contact and engage in more personal disclosure in the course of their business together. This disclosure may involve private thoughts and feelings about work-related matters or it may pertain to aspects of their private lives. Low-distance managers argue that such personal contact improves decision making, performance, and motivation. They tend to believe that the whole person comes to work and that a close relationship improves the quality of their work lives.

On the other hand, managers who prefer to maintain a more businesslike or arm's-length approach to the relationship have a high-distance style. They believe that more work can be done because less time is consumed talking about things that are not immediately and obviously relevant to the task at hand. They like a "no-nonsense," task-oriented approach and argue that it helps them be more objective, avoid role confusion, and keep their work and personal lives separate. They also feel there is less political vulnerability in this orientation, because there is less chance that personal information might be used against them.

Divergence

Divergence asks the question: How important is it for me to protect myself? Should I assume our goals are aligned, our methods are alike, and my boss is my ally, not my competitor or even my adversary?

Subordinate managers with an orientation to low divergence assume there is a close alignment between themselves and their bosses over legitimate goals and the means for achieving those goals. They also believe that people in authority are concerned with balancing the subordinate's goals and interests with their own interests, as well as those of the organization. Such a subordinate manager sees no need to be concerned with self-protection in the relationship with authority. The boss is seen as an ally who can be trusted.

Subordinate managers with an orientation to high divergence, on the other hand, tend to see the boss as a competitor or adversary and are likely to mistrust the boss or others in positions of authority. They see the relation to authority as one that is very likely to involve divergence over goals and over the means for achieving them. Such managers assume that the boss is preoccupied with narrow or selfish interests and is concerned with neither the subordinate's interests nor (in the extreme) the organization's interests. This kind of high-divergence orientation thus leads to a relationship that is framed in adversarial terms.

How the Factors Combine

Deference, distance, and divergence are the factors that make up subordinate style, but they do not occur in isolation. They are combined in different ways. Also, managers' beliefs are seldom as clear cut as the pure types would suggest. A manager might score high or low on one or two factors but in the middle on the third. Or the manager might tend toward the high or low range of all three, but not be at the extreme ends in any case. In other words, managers combine deference, distance, and divergence in differing amounts or with varying intensity.

These score patterns (different ways of combining the three factors) make up the variations in the ways managers approach relationships with bosses. For example, take the case of a manager who believes the boss should make the decisions and he should defer (high deference), that the relationship with the boss should be no-nonsense and businesslike (high distance), and that there is little difference in the boss's goals and his own and that the boss has his best interests at heart (low divergence). This style is found quite frequently in business organizations, government, and the military. It makes up what I call the Military style.

One of the useful things about this way of looking at the boss-subordinate relationship is the way we can understand more about managers who have a certain style and how they are likely to view their relationships with authority. Managers with the Military style, for example, are likely to go along with the boss and see their primary responsibility as support and implementation. They will be direct and to the point in conversations with the boss. If they do not understand why a certain decision has been made, they are likely to assume it is a good decision and that, if they had all the facts, they would make the same decision. It is a matter of having the same goals and trusting the boss.

Or take another, quite different, style. This manager wants a lot of influence (low deference), wants a very close and personal relationship with her bosses (low distance), and, while she sees some difference in her own goals and those of her bosses, also sees them as generally supportive (in the middle on divergence). I call this the Counselor style.

Counselor-style managers are generally more senior and have a strong sense of their own expertise. They often occupy staff roles. There are more women than men in this group. (An interesting note here is that, although statistics show that men and women are not different in any consistent way on the factors of distance and divergence, women are significantly less deferential than men; women, more often than men and with greater persistence, push for influence with their bosses.)

Finally, here is a style I call the Rebel. Managers with this style push back hard on the boss and do not like to implement decisions they had no role in making (low deference). They tend to create a more personal relationship that helps them in trying to influence the boss (low distance). Yet they do not fully trust the boss, and so they are self-protective (high divergence). As we will see in more detail later, Rebels tend to be younger, quite well educated, and relatively low in the managerial hierarchy. There are a lot of them in education and social services, fewer in business, health care, and government.

Examining the three aspects (deference, distance, and divergence) at three levels of intensity (high, low, medium) revealed nine subordinate styles that occur regularly in organizations. As I conducted a more in-depth analysis of these styles, I found I could group them according to three basic orientations: accommodating approaches, autonomous approaches, and adversarial approaches.

- *Accommodating styles* are those in which the subordinate manager generally works as a support to those in authority, staying within the structure provided. There are four accommodating styles: Military, Helper, Diplomat, and Partisan.
- *Autonomous styles* are those in which the subordinates work apart from, or avoid, authority, and prefer to create their own structure within broad guidelines. There are two autonomous styles: the Counselor and the Independent.
- *Adversarial styles* are those in which the subordinate works in opposition to the authority, and resists or even tries to smash the structure. There are three: the Gamesman, the Rebel, and the Whistleblower.

We will see later how each style offers useful variations in approach to authority relationships, and how each has its advantages and disadvantages. But first, we will look at each of the three main factors of deference, distance, and divergence in more detail, so that we will be better able to understand the styles themselves and how they can be usefully varied to make relationships with authority more effective.

Chapter Two

Sharing Power with Your Boss: Questions of Deference

> The President doesn't want any yes-men and yes-women around him. When he says no, we all say no.
>
> —*Elizabeth Dole*

Do you often push back against your boss? Are you often quick (perhaps the first) to state what should be done? Do you frequently assume the devil's advocate role in conversations with your boss? Do you find yourself taking up a lot of air time in meetings with your boss? Do you suspect (or know) that your boss sees you as contentious, argumentative? Do you often feel an urgent need to convince your boss that you are right? Is it difficult for you to accept and support decisions you do not agree with? Do you then find it hard to let go of your investment in your preferred outcome? Do you feel troubled that your boss is attracted to all the trappings of status?

If you answered yes to some or all of these, or if you leaned toward a yes answer, it suggests that you have an orientation to low deference.

Do you prefer structure and clear lines of authority? In meetings with your boss, do you take the position that, if asked, you will offer your view, but otherwise you are not inclined to volunteer? Do you assume that your expertise or understanding concerning a particular problem or decision is not often very valuable to your boss? Does your boss rarely recognize your skill or expertise? Do you spend a lot of time thinking about how to deliver certain kinds of information to your boss? Do you spend a lot of time preparing reports and presentations for your boss? Do you subject your own views to rigorous (private) reflection and scrutiny before you discuss them in a open forum? Do you only infrequently pose your ideas and suggestions? Does your boss not seem to hear your views or take them seriously? Do you tend to withhold your views until you get a sense of what the boss wants (or expects) to hear?

If you answered yes to some or all of these, or of you leaned toward yes, it suggests that you have an orientation to high deference.

About Deference

Deference is related to the subordinate's primary focus of attention. A low-deference person is more directed toward her own thoughts and ideas, is likely to feel that it is a primary responsibility of those in subordinate roles to push for influence in the decision-making process. Her internal voices speak more loudly and persistently than those of external authority. This manager could be considered inner-directed.

On the other hand, the manager who gives more consideration to the boss's judgments and ideas is more likely to see his role as primarily a support to the boss and an effective implementer of the boss's plans. High-deference managers grant more consideration to the boss's views than to their own.

By thinking about yourself in these terms, you may be beginning already to form some reasonable conclusions about your own orientation to deference. Later in this chapter I will discuss each orientation in detail, including the strengths and weaknesses of each approach. First, however, I want to take a little detour to discuss where these kinds of orientations come from and what inputs make up a style, so that you can better understand the power of your style and why you may feel so attached to it. I then want to address briefly an issue that is frequently raised when people first start to think about their own style: the difference between behavior and underlying attitudes and values.

Formation of Style

According to an article in the *Wall Street Journal*, Colonel Oliver North's motivation for his Iran-Contra involvement was in no small part due to "a lifelong desire to work hard to please his superiors" (Greenberger and Langley, 1986, p. 1). Some of North's family members linked this desire with what they described as a warm and affectionate relationship with his late father, a decorated World War II veteran, who apparently influenced North heavily in his choice of career. In addition, North had a history of good relationships with other authority figures, such as coaches and teachers. "Friends and former colleagues paint a picture of a man who throughout his life has nurtured a series of close relationships with male authority figures. . . . To many of these men, Oliver North—college boxing champion, war hero, and fast track Marine officer—was the perfect surrogate son" (p. 1).

Where does a person's orientation toward authority come from? People are often curious about how such an orientation forms. How does someone come to have a particular style in approach to deference?

As Oliver North's story suggests, our orientation toward authority has its beginnings in the family of origin, with our first authorities: parents. This is the classical Freudian view. It says that our so-called primary socialization in the family establishes our orientation. Some even argue that this is the major or even sole determiner of orientation and that it sets the pattern for life. Such a view sees the approach to authority relationships as "hard wired" into personality and very difficult (if not impossible) to change.

My view is different. I believe style is something we learn. Certainly this learning begins in the family, but it does not end there. It continues well into adulthood and is continually being shaped by our exposure and reactions to ongoing experiences.

The classical Freudian view fails to consider two other forces, which I believe play an important role. The primary socialization in the family is followed by secondary socialization in schools and organizations, particularly large-scale organizations. We learn to yield to, and to work with, our teachers in schools; later, we learn how to get along with our bosses at work. In addition there is the powerful effect of the media and our constant exposure to its messages. Thus family, schools and organizations, and the media all play a part in our learning an approach to authority. In Freud's time, his view of the family as the crucible that shapes us made sense. However, he did not experience and could not have predicted the effects of these other forces—especially the media.[1]

While most of us may be somewhat aware of the influence that our work life and our earlier schooling have on us, we may be almost completely unaware of how powerful the impressions are that we take away from our constant exposure to television and other media. We are bombarded with information and images daily that further shape our orientation to certain beliefs about how people in authority use (and abuse) their power.

For example, when a president of the United States abuses his authority, we are greeted daily in direct ways with who was involved, how they did it, what they thought and said. As I write this, there is a story in the news of how one of President Clinton's aides took a presidential helicopter to go play golf. While in most senses a minor issue, it has received a great deal of attention in the media. It is generally being cast as the typical abuse of privilege and power we have witnessed frequently.

Such exposure goes a long way to shape and reinforce beliefs about how people in authority handle themselves. Of course, the corollary to this is a lesson about how we, as subordinates, must handle ourselves in relation to that authority.

Out of these three experience inputs (family, organizations, media) we develop a set of beliefs about authority and our relation to it. These beliefs are not hard-wired. Like all beliefs, they are changeable. But like many beliefs, they tend not to change because the inputs that help form them are often quite consistent. We keep getting the same messages over and over, and we keep interpreting them in the same ways. This process grooves our beliefs into a pattern, a style, that is reinforced through typical organizational ways of operating, career paths, and the fact that we do little systematic learning about ourselves in the authority relationship.

Style then becomes durable, and it tends to persist. If we are confronted with data or information that contradicts our beliefs, we tend to reject the new information or we reshape it to allow us to hold onto our existing beliefs. Style preferences can thus be quite persistent.

Overt Behavior, Underlying Convictions

At this point you may be wondering, as a lot of people do, whether you really do have a durable style in your relationships with authority. Many people tell me that they change their approach to authority depending on the particular boss they have. So what is all this about an enduring style?

My answer is that people's *behavior* in their approach to authority may very well change depending on who the boss is and what the boss's own style may be. However, people's underlying attitudes and beliefs about what is proper, appropriate, and desirable do not change as readily. They are more consistent and persistent over time.

Assume, for example, that I believe strongly that I have something to contribute to my boss's decision-making process. This conviction is likely to become a persistent preference, an element of my style. However, my boss, it turns out, is an autocratic manager. He does not seek or allow for my input or influence. He values only my skills at implementing decisions—decisions I have had no part in shaping. It is likely that outwardly, behaviorally, I will comply. Whether I do this out of fear of punishment or a sense of duty, I will probably try to accommodate to my boss. Even though it goes against the grain, I will adapt and act the role of the executive implementer.

However, it is unlikely that I will change my underlying attitudes or belief system (style preference) about what *should* be happening when decisions are made. And the contrast between my beliefs and my behavior is likely to create tension in me and in the relationship with the boss. To a greater or lesser degree, the relationship will be a source of irritation and tension.

Subordinate managers often say they make such adjustments out of necessity, to be able to work well with a boss. Yet this approach pretty much guarantees the pair will always have difficulties. Making outward adjustments in behavior so that one can work well with a boss is essentially a pursuit of comfort rather than effectiveness. This is unfortunate, since it means that a boss and a subordinate manager are often doing little more than looking for ways to get comfortable with each other when style differences appear.

Actually, it is more important that the pair decide what sort of relationship best supports their effectiveness in working on tasks. If they have a creative task that relies on an energetic give-and-take, then the subordinate manager should be pushing back, and the boss should learn how to deal with it. If they are in a crisis and quick action is necessary, then the subordinate manager should act the role of the implementer, the good soldier.

In other words, determine the requirements of the task, then adjust to that. This may involve both parties' being uncomfortable for the sake of effectiveness. Effectiveness is more important than comfort.

Attitudes toward deference must also be placed on a continuum of appropriateness to the situation. In the United States, people tend to imbue low deference with a positive connotation and high deference with a negative one. But in fact there are advantages and disadvantages associated with each approach. We will first discuss the low-deference orientation, that of being more inner-directed and pushing for influence with your boss. Then we will discuss the advantages of the high-deference orientation, or accommodating your boss. Finally, we will look at the disadvantages of each, because, depending on when or where it is used, each can be a strength or a liability.

Overview of Low Deference

Ahmed, a manager in international construction who rates low on deference, makes a simple assertion based on the logic of being inner-directed.

> I pursue strongly what I believe could and should be done. I insist on having a say in decision making and often question directions received. I prefer to work with a superior who is open to influence [and] . . . I like to see that my opinion is integrated in the ultimate decision.

Another manager, Michael, an inner-directed executive, captures several themes that are often expressed by low-deference managers.

> My attitude is, tell me what the goals are and get the heck out of the way. If I have to explain and get permission from my boss every time I want to make a move, he doesn't need me, he can have the department. Luckily, my current boss knows that while I may attack his every move to his face and in private, I will defend him and carry out his wishes (if his wishes make sense). I will and have refused to pursue paths which he has directed me to take but that I feel are an economic or ethical mistake for the company. I am always up front and honest in these situations and to date, he has respected my views and not tried to force me into a corner. When this day happens, I will do what I feel is right but will not compromise my deep-seated convictions.

Low deference is often associated with certain recurring themes, including the application of democratic ideals to the workplace, a belief in the power of knowledge and expertise, and the need for autonomy.

One common characteristic of an inner-directed, low-deference orientation is a discomfort with many of the customary trappings of authority, such as status symbols and other special privileges. At the extremes, some low-deference subordinates can resent any accentuation of the higher status of those in authority. In their view, deference means loss of dignity; the act of deference is equated with playing politics and even with so-called kissing up. They consider deference as an affront to their democratic ideals of equality. They may profess a belief that everyone should be equal and that it is somehow wrong for one person to be set higher than another in an organizational hierarchy. Such beliefs, whatever their merits, would obviously be associated with low deference.

A perhaps more common idea associated with low deference is the notion that superior expertise or knowledge in a special area gives weight and importance to judgments and ideas. Managers who hold this notion usually have a strong base of knowledge from which to operate, and they believe their opinions should carry weight. This could be one reason that higher educational credentials are generally associated with lower deference to authority, particularly up through the master's degree. These low-deference managers want not only to be heard but also to be heeded. They have an investment in seeing that a decision touching their area of expertise reflects their input.

Another frequent theme in low-deference managers is the need for autonomy. Michael may have been expressing this theme when he said he wanted his boss to "get the heck out of the way." Many managers see themselves as having something unique to contribute that cannot be contributed if the boss is going to get too involved. Low-deference managers of this kind may be indicating deep investment and involvement in the job or a passionate feeling about the issues at hand. They may also feel impatient and ready to assume more responsibility and authority themselves.

Then there are some low-deference managers who are, for whatever reasons, simply resistant to *any* form of external guidance. They tend to see any direction and structure from the boss as an unwarranted intrusion on their professional or personal autonomy. The relationship in this case can become quite strained, often involving control struggles between the subordinate manager and the boss.

Not all low-deference subordinates push for influence before decisions get made. Although Michael, for example, feels quite strongly that his boss should get out of the way, he does grant that his boss has legitimate decision-making powers.

> I have always felt that my superior should have the power which is necessary for him to accomplish the items which make good business sense. If a tough decision must be made, he has that right, but he must explain his reasoning to me.

Michael is thus willing to support decisions made without his involvement if, after the decision has been made, the reasoning behind the decision is made clear.

Other managers, such as Frank, are especially attuned to the appropriateness of contexts in which to push for influence with the boss.

> One thing I have learned is to support my superior's final decision actively, even when I do not personally agree with it. I will aggressively argue in private, but in meetings I am careful to actively support my boss.

This distinction between public and private deference is made by some low-deference managers, like Frank, who recognize that relationships can be poisoned by continuing resistance in public after a decision is made. Their pushing for influence in the decision-making process thus has self-imposed limits.

Managers from functions concerned with change, or ones that push the organization and act like an organizational conscience, tend toward low deference. These would include human resources and quality control. Marketing and sales is in something of a middle category but has more in common with the low-deference functions than the high-deference ones.

Advantages of Low Deference

As we have seen, low deference comes in different forms. What are the advantages of a low-deference style? What do low-deference managers bring to the relationship and to the decision-making process? If you are beginning to see yourself as having a low-deference orientation, what advantages could you expect to bring to your organization and to the relationship with your boss?

If you are a low-deference subordinate, you exhibit the following characteristics:

- You are willing to advocate ideas, including new and sometimes even unpopular ideas.
- You usually make it easy for your boss to know where you stand.
- You are not reluctant to find and reveal the flaws in proposals. You are willing to be the devil's advocate.
- You are not constrained by a need to agree with the boss; you are often creative and innovative; you are not a conformist.
- You are quite able, and often prefer, to work under loose supervision and to be relatively autonomous.
- You lend an energy and liveliness to your work and to the relationship with your boss.
- You often feel eager and ready to assume more responsibility.

Thus, low deference makes sense when you, the subordinate manager, feel you have solid expertise (or knowledge) that bears on matters under consideration, or when you feel that there is a wrong, unethical, or even dangerous plan under consideration. It can also be useful when innovation and creativity are called for and when you are being required to operate under autonomous work conditions.

Other conditions also need to be present for the low-deference style and the relative subordinate autonomy it implies to be most effective. These include such things as timely, accurate information; a broad base of knowledge about and appreciation of corporate and subunit goals; and specified points of contact with other workers and functions. Strongly inner-directed, low-deference managers may need to be reminded that they are operating in a cooperative context. Organizational coordination often requires modifying individual preferences and actions for the sake of overall (particularly cross-functional) progress.

To sum up: Low deference can lead to better decision processes, increased consideration of different viewpoints, more scrutiny of the do-ability of a solution, and increased assurance of integrity. It can also assist in the development of the subordinate manager and provide an indicator of readiness to assume higher-level responsibilities.

Overview of High Deference

George, a contracts attorney in a high-technology company, characterizes the high-deference style well.

> My boss is not an attorney. He has, however, worked in my field for many years—the last fifteen of which have been at our company. Our relationship is quite open . . . and my preference is for a relatively personal, nonadversarial relationship. . . . I have no problem with symbols and accessories traditionally associated with positions of status. I'm generally comfortable with behind-the-scenes activity in support of my supervisors' positions on issues. I don't defer to my boss on issues of technical skill where I am clearly educated and trained to be the greater authority. I do, however, realize that many decisions are

made on other than purely technical matters and that my boss has access to information that I do not. We are not in competition with each other. In general . . . Jack and I are very compatible.

Like the low-deference style, high deference has its own logic. Many of the themes of this logic are alluded to in George's description of his relationship with his boss, including a preference for clear lines of authority in the organization, a preference for working within well-defined structures, and an appreciation of the multiple criteria by which any proposed action should be judged. Just as the low-deference orientation arises from an inner-directed interest in one's own ideas, the high-deference style comes from having a relatively high consideration of the ideas and judgments of others, especially those of people in authority.

The high-deference orientation can be described as that of the good soldier, a person whose main interest is in carrying out plans and decisions made by those with more authority and knowledge. This person is comfortable not having input or influence in decisions; he is not particularly troubled if his views are not reflected in the ultimate decision. Such an orientation is often accompanied by a comfort with large power disparities and with the status symbols and trappings that normally surround authority and powerful bosses.

A common facet of the high-deference orientation is discomfort with unstructured problems and ambiguous decision situations. These managers prefer clearer connections between the ends and the means used to achieve them. Frequently, high-deference subordinates prefer structured problems and like to leave the muddier issues to their bosses. Thus, a typical high-deference manager may say that she feels more comfortable in an organization where there are clear lines of authority.

This must not be misunderstood. A high-deference orientation is not an unthinking, acquiescent posture. Rather, for those who prefer it, there is often an articulated logic and usually a clear sense of personal competence that is distinct from the boss's competence.

Such managers often indicate a preference for a boss who is forceful, perhaps even charismatic, and who, by making most of the decisions and judgments, helps the subordinates concentrate on a special area of expertise.

As we saw in George's comments, the high-deference style sometimes revolves around an appreciation of the fact that non-technical considerations are frequently driving the decision process. Managers like George understand that their technical expertise, while relevant, may not be the paramount consideration in many decision situations. Other considerations may assume greater importance: organizational strategy and goals; tactical considerations; political issues (the most technically elegant solution may not be do-able or politically feasible); costs and other budgetary considerations; and interdepartmental equity.

Managers from the more technical areas in business organizations tend toward high deference. High-deference managers are disproportionately represented in engineering, finance, and accounting. Production and manufacturing managers tend to be more represented in the high-deference group as well. The high-deference group has a disproportionately low representation from human resource and quality control managers.

Advantages of High Deference

The high-deference approach to the authority relationship has a number of positive aspects for the boss, the organization, and for the subordinate manager. If you see yourself in the description of the high-deference approach, what benefits could you expect to bring to your organization and to the relationship with your boss?

If you have a high-deference orientation, you exhibit the following characteristics:

- You are usually a good implementer; you accept direction easily; you contribute by making things happen.

- You are open to new information; you are not usually defensive about what you do not know. You may bring new information into the organization.

- You do not take up valuable time discussing and arguing before getting to action; this is especially important in a crisis.

- Your energy in the boss-subordinate relationship is mostly devoted to getting the work done; you are not often distracted by power and influence issues, because you tend to accept the reality and inequality of power differences.

- You generally create smoother, more trusting boss-subordinate relationships.[2]

- You generally accept that decisions cannot always be made with reference to technical criteria alone, and you are content to leave to the boss the muddier, more ambiguous issues of politics, priorities, and so on.

In addition to these advantages, the subordinate manager with a high-deference approach may get a lot of appreciation from a boss who feels well supported. This is particularly true when the high-deference manager fulfills not only the letter of the boss's directives but the spirit as well. The view of this subordinate as a solid citizen will probably incline the boss to be a strong sponsor and may facilitate a mentoring relationship.

An interesting side note is that high-deference managers often report less work stress and more success at keeping their work and private lives separate.

One issue in career development for this manager is whether to choose a technical career path or one in management. The management career track may bring a high-deference manager face to face with just those elements of organizational life—ambiguity, political give and take, fuzzy, indeterminate problems—that he prefers to avoid. This is not to suggest that he does not have the personality for management, only that certain organizational realities can push him out of his comfort zone.

The Flip Side: Disadvantages

We have seen how both low- and high-deference approaches to the relationship with authority can be advantageous to the individual and the organization. But any strength, if used inappropriately or to excess, can become a liability.

The low-deference approach—pushing for influence—can help in making good decisions. However, if carried too far, it can become an obstruction; it creates an adversarial tone in the boss-subordinate relationship and damages the pair's effectiveness. Such was apparently the case between Abraham Lincoln and General George B. McClellan during the American Civil War. McClellan, commanding the Army of the Potomac, was notorious for his refusal to defer to anyone in authority over him.[3]

It was at a critical point in the war, just after the battle of Antietam (Sharpsburg) in September 1862. Earlier, during the single bloodiest day of the war, McClellan had succeeded in severely weakening Lee's Army of Northern Virginia. After a day of waiting in place for a renewed attack, Lee had withdrawn back across the Potomac. McClellan had allowed him to escape.

At that moment the Union forces under McClellan had a tremendous advantage and an opportunity to attack Lee's army again and finish the war there and then. Lincoln had repeatedly insisted that McClellan do this, and he continued to press for this attack. McClellan, pushing back on his boss's authority, protested that he had achieved his aims because he had "driven the enemy from our soil." An apoplectic Lincoln shot back: "It is *all* our soil!" Lincoln knew, but could never convince his top generals (until Grant), that the war was not about taking and holding land. The war would go on until Lee's army surrendered. Had McClellan done what Lincoln demanded of him, the war might have ended two years before it did, saving thousands of lives.

On the other hand, when being the good soldier is carried too far, high deference can become collusion. The subordinate's critical judgment can be suspended, bringing suboptimal, unethical, or even dangerous decisions.

After the *Challenger* shuttle disaster, the Rogers Commission identified one of the central problems that led to the explosion: "the difficulty in relaying to the top concerns raised at the lower levels." Physicist Richard Feynman, a commission member, said, "Things were happening lower down . . . and the guys higher up didn't know . . . they kept being shocked and surprised." Feynman was asked why the information did not flow to the top. Was it a failure of procedures? He replied that "the disease was larger and more pervasive" throughout the cultures at NASA and Morton-Thiokol. He said the reason communication did not flow upward was that lower-level managers were afraid to confront their bosses with the truth (Feynman, 1988, p. 215). High deference to authority, particularly characteristic of engineering-driven organizational cultures, thus worked to suppress the transmission of critical information.

Here are some dangers you may face as a low-deference subordinate manager.

1. *Pushing your boss past any useful point.* This will only alienate your boss and will reduce, not enhance, your prospects for influence (not to mention what it might do to your career prospects). When a subordinate pursues disagreement past the point of decision, the boss is likely to erect defensive barriers. Be sure your pushing back is appropriate to the stage of decision making. As the decision process converges on implementation, that may not be the right time to reopen the decision premises. Consider a private one-on-one meeting with your boss. Choose your battles. Perhaps suggesting some form of follow-up evaluation of decision outcomes makes more sense.

2. *Failing to recognize that you lack information and do not see the problem in its full complexity.* Before launching an all-out attack on your boss's decision, you may need to ask if you have all the information your boss does. An important basis for your boss's authority is her location in an information network. You may not see everything or recognize fully the priorities and criteria that must be served by the outcome. Thomas Jefferson (not a bad thinker on the issue of relationships to authority) once commented, "I shall often go wrong through defect of judgment." But he added, "When right, I shall often be thought wrong by those whose positions will not command a view of the whole ground" (Mapp, 1987, p. 400).

3. *Using up large amounts of meeting time to the exclusion of others.* If you spend more time listening (truly listening) you may hear something that will alter your view. Find out if others feel pushed out of the conversation when you get engaged with your boss. Get feedback from others.

4. *Not seeking help or resources when you need them.* If you habitually disagree with your boss and make your boss's life difficult, you may gain some measure of power and autonomy but lose access to critical resources that your boss controls: information, access to higher management and decision levels, resources of various kinds, and feedback.

5. *Sabotage of decisions with which you do not agree.* This sabotage can be passive or active, and can take the form of inaction, action different from that which was directed, or seeking allies to oppose your boss. In certain situations you may feel morally compelled to do this, but carefully examine your own motives. Do not be deluded about the relationship costs with your boss once such actions become known. Opt, whenever possible, for more direct ways to handle differences.

6. *Pushing back for the wrong reasons.* Some people may relive old struggles with authority figures from the past (parents, teachers)

or with people in the present (spouses). Remember that your boss is your boss, not your father or mother. Do not make decision making an arena for personal power struggles. Also, listen to yourself. Note with concern a tendency to habitually negate without putting in something new. You will use up, and waste, a lot of personal and organizational resources.

As a low-deference manager, when you take a different view, ground your view for others in different data that you might have or a clearly detailed reasoning process built on different assumptions or values. This will keep the focus on the problem to be solved or the decision to be made. At least some of the time, consider hanging back with your concerns to see if others will raise them. You may have "trained" your co-workers to wait for you to pose the contrarian view in meetings, encouraging them to withhold their concerns in the expectation that you will do all the necessary challenging. Ask that devil's advocates other than yourself be appointed. Also seek feedback regularly from your co-workers and your boss as to whether you are seen as thoughtful and cooperative or contentious and argumentative.

Here are some dangers you may face as a high-deference subordinate manager.

1. *Limited advancement on a management track.* If you are too high in deference to authority, you may end up being thought of as someone without a lot of leadership potential, as someone who lacks fire and energy. This may not be important to you if you are on a technical career track and have few leadership or general management aspirations.

2. *A tendency to go along with bad decisions.* Excessive or habitual high deference can stop a manager from even questioning whether this decision is good or bad, ethical or unethical, safe or dangerous.

3. *Lack of appreciation of your contributions.* If you have a tendency to be unduly modest about your own knowledge, skills, and experiences, your boss may think less of these things. If you telegraph this modesty to others, it may signal to them that your input is not worthwhile or that it is acceptable for people to ignore your ideas. This lack of appreciation may hurt your self-esteem and discourage you from injecting new or different ideas into the decision-making process. You are likely to end up making a much smaller contribution than you could have.

4. *Pursuing comfort at the expense of effectiveness.* A certain amount of creative tension in boss-subordinate relationships can be quite useful. And an excessive concern for avoiding controversy and conflict can become dangerous. Many high-deference subordinates confuse a boss's charm and charisma with competence, values, and appropriate motivation. Some conflict with the boss is bound to be necessary for effectiveness, because no one person can ever have all the right answers.

In general, if you are a high-deference manager you may need to push yourself to speak up, particularly when the problem or decision is in your professional bailiwick. If not, learn to ask good questions. The role of the naive questioner can effectively prod bosses and groups to question themselves and their understandings.

It is imperative for all good managers to learn how to balance their approach with its opposite. A low-deference, inner-directed manager needs to learn how and when to give greater consideration to the ideas and judgments of the boss—to defer. Likewise, the high-deference manager needs to learn how and when to stand up for his own ideas and judgments and push back against the boss.

Chapter Three

Being Up Close and Personal
with Your Boss:
Issues of Distance

The issue of personal distance hit home for me. I do
believe that subordinates and superiors should have
the ability to be personal and professional at the
same time. The individuals who work for me
understand that I will be very open and friendly with
them but when *work time comes, work time comes.*
— *An executive in the research project*

'Tis distance lends enchantment to the view,
and robes the mountain in its azure hue.
— *Thomas Campbell,* Pleasures of Hope, *1799*

Does conversation of a personal nature consume a lot of your interaction time with your boss? Do you feel that your work relationships, particularly the one with your boss, are for social contact as
well? Do you talk with your boss about your aspirations, dreams,
fears, or anxieties? Are you often eager to tell your boss of events,
successes, concerns in your personal life apart from work? Have you
and your boss jointly created some plans for your development?
Does your boss know about, and consider in her assignments and
outcome expectations, relevant facets of your private life such as
childbirth, marriage, death of a loved one, divorce, or illness? Do
you sometimes feel overexposed or vulnerable because of personal
information your boss has about you?

If you answered yes to some or all of these questions, or if you leaned toward a yes answer, it suggests that you have an orientation to low distance.

Do you believe that a boss-subordinate relationship should be kept friendly but businesslike and objective? Are you uncomfortable if the boss discloses or reveals some aspects of his private life to you? Do you prefer to separate your social life and relationships from your work? Do a boss's inquiries about your personal life make you wary and uncomfortable? Do you think such interest is an invasion of your privacy and inappropriate? Do you harbor fears that personal disclosure in this relationship will be used to your detriment? Do you prefer a boss who maintains a certain distance? Should contact between a boss and a subordinate manager be limited to work-related matters?

If you answered yes to some or all of these questions, or if you leaned toward a yes answer, it suggests that you have an orientation to high distance.

About Distance

Distance in the boss-subordinate relationship is related to how personal and open the two people prefer to be with each other. If a manager feels that it is appropriate and desirable to establish and maintain personal contact with the boss and that such contact is important, then she would be considered more personally oriented (low distance). Managers of this type feel that openness and being personal are in themselves rewarding, and that this kind of relationship enriches work and makes the boss-subordinate pair more effective. They believe that the relationship exists primarily between two people, two human beings; the role differences are secondary, perhaps in the background.

If, on the other hand, a manager feels that, while being friendly is important, personal contact in the relationship is unnecessary, interferes with objectivity, and is not businesslike, he would be considered more role oriented (high distance.) Although managers with this preference may have many rewarding personal relationships outside work, they do not consider personal contact between boss and subordinate as rewarding. Instead, they feel that it tends to consume time, makes the manager vulnerable, and clouds the work relationship. Furthermore, it blurs the line between work and personal life. To these managers, the boss-subordinate relationship should be governed by role definitions; personal contact is a distraction and an intrusion.

The Formation of Distance Orientation

People look to their work for many different things. Motivation theorists have, for a long time, recognized that the list of rewards includes economic security, status, direction, and structure. It also includes social contact, or affiliation. One theory even elevates this social need to one of three basic drives, the other two being a need for achievement and a need for power (McClelland and Burnham, 1991).

It is often said that the whole person comes to work, that we cannot help but arrive at work each day with our needs, hopes, wishes, fears, and concerns. But, while we share common characteristics and interests in this respect, each of us handles them differently, choosing to pursue or deny, share or withhold, aspects of ourselves with our co-workers.

Development theories suggest that we all have predispositions about how to handle this need. Like other aspects of style, our way of handling it has beginnings in our early life. These preferences are further shaped, reinforced, and possibly changed through early and later adulthood. Some people develop so as to meet this need primarily outside the workplace and do not much value social connection at work. Others value social contact at work a great deal and invest a lot of energy in pursuing and maintaining personal contact.

Managers can thus be characterized by the degree to which they pursue affiliation, or personal contact, in their work relations. The orientation toward distance is emphasized in the boss-subordinate relationship. Research has shown that, compared to all their other work relationships, managers tend to be the least disclosing to their bosses. For some managers, then, who have relatively little interest in pursuing this form of contact anyway, the relationship with those in authority is maintained as a relatively distant one in a personal sense. They usually place some value on being cordial and friendly but keep personal disclosure at a minimum. Other managers, perhaps with greater need for closeness in general, may have modest interest in having a personal relationship with the boss and some openness to personal disclosure. It is not always sought, nor is it always expected to be two-way disclosure, but nonetheless it is there in moderate amounts.

For still others, the need for closeness is highly developed, and the work environment is a primary source of personal contact. They prize the opportunity to work with people they like and the opportunity to get close to the people they work with. In these times of downsizing and retrenchment, when work seems to require so many more hours than in the past, more and more people are being forced to satisfy their social needs in this way. Managers in this last category, consciously or unconsciously, use their work involvement as a way to develop a personal relationship with the boss. It is, for them, an integral part of their reward structure.

People from human resources, sales, and marketing seem more oriented to personalizing relationships, being more outgoing and gregarious, while those in accounting and engineering are less so. In the data from this research, such attributions are supported. On the distance scale, human resource managers score quite low, indicating a preference for personalizing the boss-subordinate relationship. Marketing managers are in the middle range with a similar, though weaker, preference. Managers in engineering and R&D score significantly higher, and those in accounting and finance, production, and manufacturing score the highest. These last groups indicate a strong preference for role orientations in their relationships with people in authority. Analysis of variance indicates, not surprisingly, that the variations are statistically significant. These are not random or accidental differences. Those managers in the more traditional technical areas prefer greater distance in their authority relationships (and probably other relationships as well).

Overview of Low Distance

In general, a low-distance orientation suggests a preference for a relationship with authority that emphasizes more personal exchange. While such a preference does not necessarily express itself in all instances or with all bosses, it does reflect a person's general leaning and preferred climate or context for carrying on with work. For these subordinates, personal exchange is a natural and important part of their work lives, one that can either be encouraged and supported by a boss or avoided and discouraged. In the latter event, there are serious risks for both the relationship and the work. For those who prefer more personal contact, its absence can be felt keenly, even to the point of leaving a job.

Janet, a product manager with a computer company, points to the great importance low-distance managers tend to attach to a more personalized boss-subordinate relationship.

> I have a good working relationship with my managers. I do enjoy a personal relationship, one in which we enjoy each other's style and are open, trusting, and honest with each other. I've always looked for this relationship with my managers. If I do not establish this relationship, I usually leave the group for a position in another group where I *can* establish this kind of working relationship.
>
> I have on many (informal) occasions discussed my feelings about the organization with my management. I enjoy these discussions because I get another perspective on what is going on in the

organization. Interesting to note is that my manager also tends to enjoy discussing the organization with me. On many occasions, my manager has stopped in my office to "gossip" about organizational information. We both tend to get our sources of information from different locations so we compare notes. I feel that this has enhanced our relationship and has put me at ease with her.

Janet's comments also refer to her increased comfort as a result of the personal contact and the result for both her and her boss in being freer, more effective, and finding more pleasure in their work together. But personal satisfaction is not the only reason low-distance managers pursue this contact. It can be an invaluable assist in accomplishing their work together. Combining their subjective impressions of and reactions to events and exchanges helps her and her boss to make better sense of organizational happenings.

Janet also highlights the important access to the organizational "backstage" that such contact can provide. It has helped her in her work *and* in her career progress. Often, low-distance subordinates will comment that in addition to a pleasing sense of connection their orientation provides and a sense of enrichment in the contact, they gain access to information and people that help them in doing their jobs and ultimately in their career progress. It also assists in dissipating the stresses that normally accompany work.

It is interesting to note that there is no significant overall scale difference between men and women in this research in their orientation to relating to their bosses—that is, whether they prefer personal or role relating. Women are no more or less likely than men to opt for more personal forms of relating to people in authority.

Chris, a manager in the aviation industry with a low-distance orientation, describes some of the emotional rewards he gets from greater personal contact.

With few exceptions, I have always had, or felt, a personal emphasis in my relationship with superiors. For whatever reason, I tend to place importance on this. It has provided me with positive and secure feelings in my professional relationships. More important, it has given me a sense of importance within the organization or group. . . . I like the feeling of personal emphasis in my relationships with my superiors and feel confident enough to handle their criticism.

Chris's comments underscore several additional themes in the low-distance approach: feelings of confidence and security engendered by a close relationship with the boss, assurance that the boss will be interested in one's development and advancement, belief that work is more easily accomplished when the relationship is close, and having a relationship cushion to support receiving critical feedback.

For these low-distance subordinates, work interactions with those in authority are most satisfying when they are complemented with more personal exchange of information. Such exchange contains information of two distinct types. One is information about the subordinate's private life. Within some limits, of course, the more personally oriented subordinate feels relatively comfortable disclosing aspects of his private thoughts—values, hopes, aspirations, dreams, disappointments—and exchanging information on the daily ebb and flow of events outside the workplace: exciting personal accomplishments, family issues, interests, avocational pursuits, significant events, and the like.

The second type of personal exchange concerns organizationally relevant happenings and their effects on the subordinate. For the subordinate with a low-distance orientation, the boss will not only hear about events but also some detail about how they affected the subordinate and how he reacted to them. The subordinate's subjective experience will be related along with descriptions of events.

Managers address the issue of personal distance in a few different ways. Some managers with a more personal orientation to the relationship with their boss prefer active and two-way disclosure. They enjoy contact where both share information about themselves and their innermost thoughts and feelings. Others appreciate the opportunity to talk about themselves and to speak openly with their bosses but are uncomfortable if the boss does likewise.

For those with a preference for charismatic bosses, and greater comfort with dependency, such disclosure by their boss tends to evoke feelings of insecurity and uncertainty. Others, most notably the Rebel group, appear to prefer the opposite. They prefer to remain somewhat concealed themselves but like it when the boss confides in them. The tactical and strategic advantages in this last practice are hard to overlook.

Advantages of Low Distance

Persuasive arguments have been made that the need for affiliation, which to varying degrees is part of most people's makeup, is more than simply its own reward—it also helps in accomplishing work (see Boyatsis, 1991). If the boss has some sense of the subordinate manager on a personal level, task accomplishment is facilitated and also motivational and developmental needs are served. For example, if the boss is going to assist in development, she needs to have some knowledge of the subordinate's hopes, dreams, aspirations, and fears. And since motivation can be considered emotional management, that same boss will need to know what stirs the manager's excitement, what creates anxiety, what causes sorrow or depression, and so on.

General knowledge (but not necessarily detail) about important life events such as childbirth, marriage, divorce, and illness can also help bosses make assignments that are more likely to produce better results. If the manager is in the midst of some personal trauma, this may not be the time, for both work and personal reasons, to send him abroad on an assignment. While some conflicts between work and personal life are probably inevitable, bosses can use their discretion in timing projects, requiring travel, and providing backup to minimize the stresses and distractions.

Research has also shown that affiliation at work increases and enhances interpersonal communication, that it helps people understand their own feelings as well as the feelings of co-workers, bosses, and subordinates. This is a vital tool in creating effective motivational climates. Managers with a high, though not extreme, need for affiliation ("affiliative interest") will strive for approval and are likely to strive for excellence in order to gain it. Such managers tend to be more adept at integrating different viewpoints and typically exert more developmental influence with co-workers and subordinates.

Further, the more affiliative manager is more likely to be open to others' influence in decision situations and to be chosen by co-workers as someone they want to work with, even when the manager is less technically competent than his colleagues. Further, when positive feelings surround work relationships, information exchange is increased and is likely to be more complete and more accurate. In these times of heightened interest in team functioning, collaborative work, creativity, and tearing down functional barriers, this orientation is likely to be important to enhance organizational competitiveness.

The low-distance orientation, then, has many advantages for the subordinate, the boss, and the organization. If you tend toward a low-distance orientation, you offer your boss, co-workers, and organization the following advantages:

- You will encourage a more complete information exchange, including subjective impressions and nuance, and more complete and effective interpretation of data.

- Your strengths and weaknesses will be better known (as will those of your boss), and it will be easier to deploy your respective talents appropriately.

- You will be able to bring out the emotional aspects in a decision and thus improve outcomes.

- You will be a better partner with your boss in task assignment and developing effective performance expectations.
- Your boss will understand better what motivates you.
- You will be more likely to enter into an effective mentoring relationship.

Overview of High Distance

As is the case with other approaches, those who adhere to a high-distance orientation offer their own logic for the approach. Contrary to a tempting stereotype, these managers do not necessarily come across as cold or impersonal. In most cases, they are friendly and approachable, just reserved in the amount of disclosure they seek and offer in the relationships with their bosses. Their approach is the outcome of their histories, their training, and often their organizational cultures.

David's is an interesting profile. His background is the U.S. Navy, his training and education are in nuclear engineering, and his current corporate responsibilities are in human resources. He scored very high on a measure of his distance orientation.

> I consider my score to be indicative of being in a highly regulated and regimented business in which many of the personnel have a military background. Due to the nature of my industry and the former Navy personnel in it, the generally expected and accepted way of doing business emphasizes distance. The emphasis on distance characterizes the relationship I have with my boss. We operate at arm's length. The relationship centers on task and goal completion. I consider my boss's style to be similar to my own, and I feel the organization's culture supports this style.

David's military background and current business affiliation help to support his orientation. These are the two most role-oriented organizational cultures, scoring the highest on the distance measures. The demands of these cultures, plus his training in engineering, suggest to David that objectivity and carefully bounded roles suit him and his situation best.

Matt, a financial analyst in the metalworking industry, and Jeremy, a chemist, allude to two of the most frequently offered rationales for a more role-oriented approach.

I have always prided myself on my detached nature. I have in the past felt that this quality lent itself to healthy objective reasoning. . . . I always considered myself to be very forthright and explicit. [Matt]

At times, I have been too open in professional situations and have divulged information I shouldn't have. I have learned that being too open can compromise myself politically, even in a small organization. This has also weakened my trust in authority. [Jeremy]

Managers who adopt a high-distance relationship with their bosses feel that it better supports objectivity in decision making and helps to keep out things that are not immediately task-related. This is particularly the case for those who come from more structured fields of knowledge such as engineering, the sciences, finance, and accounting.

Also, as Jeremy points out, organizations are, at least in part, political systems. Since personal disclosure can be used to a manager's detriment, the high-distance orientation can help to minimize exposure and vulnerability. High-distance managers also believe that because less time is taken up discussing personal things, this approach is more efficient. In contrast, one low-distance manager complained that it took him and his boss a half hour to cover five minutes' worth of work.

High-distance managers also say they see their roles more clearly, because task and personal boundaries are kept clearer and less cluttered. This last characteristic is one often mentioned by women, who express understandable concerns about maintaining the boundary between their work and personal relationships. Many women managers are concerned that even appropriate personal disclosure will be misunderstood or interpreted as an invitation to other forms of intimacy.

Another reason managers have for favoring more distance in the relationship with the boss is to avoid complicating performance assessments. Strategically, it appears to be the wise posture to assume, since appraisals are then based on measurable performance toward specific goals.

It is not only work efficiency, time, and political safety that prompt these managers to maintain more of a role-oriented relationship. It also helps many managers to maintain their privacy and a boundary between their work lives and their personal lives. Stephen, an engineering manager comments:

> I work quite hard; therefore when I go home, I don't want anything from work to interfere with my family life. So, I don't get involved with work associates (at any level).

Sadru, an engineering manager in a high-technology company, feels it is a matter of privacy.

> On personal distance, I see myself as one who emphasizes the role orientation. I do not actively seek a relationship at a personal level with my superior. It is partly because I am shy, because I respect my own privacy and feel others like the same, and also because I feel I can be more objective if I am not too "thick" with someone. I realize that this approach may lock me out of the informal channels which exist in every organization.

As more organizations find it in their interest to develop more flexible and less formal working environments and relationships, there will likely be a movement toward greater personalizing of boss-subordinate relationships. As autonomy and discretion are pushed downward in organizations to make them more responsive and adaptive, managers will increasingly operate in semiautonomous fashion. Their decisions will need to be guided by general goals and objectives, and they will need to be more adept at intuiting the intentions and values upper-level managers want to see enacted through decisions. In this development process, mentoring and sponsoring relationships will also be important, again suggesting less personal distance in boss-subordinate relationships.

However, it would be a mistake to assume this is necessary and desirable in all boss-subordinate relationships, decision situations, and organizations. This form of relating takes time and energy—both scarce resources that should be spent wisely. When time is pressing, when emotional facts are less relevant to the problem situation, and when development is not at issue, a stronger role orientation makes sense.

Management research has also pointed out that two forces in business organizations tend to work against more personalized contact in the boss-subordinate relationship. One involves mobility: where job assignments are temporary and transfers frequent, managers will tend not to form close relationships. This is especially true in military organizations. The other force is organizational politics. There is likely to be increased competition for higher-level jobs during downsizing. As Neilsen and Gypen (1979) commented, "Relating to the superior as an individual opens the door to expressing one's feelings of competition, self-doubt, dependence, and inferiority. But owning up to these feelings in a business relationship could easily be interpreted as a sign of weakness" (p. 140).

Advantages of High Distance

High distance has its own unique advantages. If you see yourself tending toward high distance, you can expect to see some or all of these benefits in your relationship with your boss:

- You will tend to promote a more objective task focus, keeping your focus on the immediate task situation.
- You will be able to approach more easily those difficult situations that might get bogged down in personal and emotional issues.
- Your interactions with the boss will use time efficiently.
- Your performance assessments are likely to be based more on measurable task outcomes.
- You will be able to promote a fuller examination of alternative problem definitions and courses of action.
- You and your boss will experience less blurring of your respective roles.
- You will find it easier to keep a sense of privacy about your personal life and maintain the boundary between your work and nonwork life.
- You will be less vulnerable to political concerns and the use of personal information.

The Flip Side: Disadvantages

Both low and high distance have their advantages, but, as we have seen with deference, anything carried to an extreme poses disadvantages, even danger.

Most managers recognize that there are dangers to too strong an interest in, or too much time devoted to, developing and maintaining relationship closeness. The principal one is that good relationships can become an end in themselves and displace task accomplishment as the primary goal. Relations can cloud the work if people develop an extreme affiliative need and become overly concerned with personal contact. These people, whom we would describe as "affiliative assurance" types, can become preoccupied with relationship quality and become grasping.

Richard Boyatsis (1991), a management researcher at Case Western Reserve University, notes, "Some individuals consistently yield to the views of the majority, and others consistently adhere to their own independent judgements. Recent research suggests that conformity tendencies may be strongest in persons who are most fearful of disapproval and rejection. People with strong affiliative needs prefer their work colleagues to be good friends, even if those friends are not very competent. Such people give priority to preserving friendly relationships, at the expense of achieving success in the group's work tasks" (p. 191).

If this occurs, too much time and energy will be devoted to the relationship itself and crucial work-related exchanges may not happen. People may simply spend too much time on purely personal matters, withhold critical feedback and opinion, avoid conflict, and even fail to disagree with their bosses.

An interesting example of the costs of fashioning close vertical relations—a personal orientation institutionalized—was the administration of President Ronald Reagan. Lou Cannon, a *Boston Globe* columnist, in 1984 wrote an editorial titled "Reagan's Excessive Loyalty." In it, he noted that Reagan "never fired anyone . . . as long as you were personally liked by the boss, you had job security." Performance was not at issue, even when it should have been. Those who confronted the president, like William Ruckelshaus of the EPA, were forced out; this did not happen often, since few were willing to risk his displeasure. Everyone said that Reagan was a truly likable person. Cannon comments, "Imagine a corporation where the least accomplished managers are rewarded and valued as much as the most productive ones. If government were truly such a corporation, it would probably be forced to seek a bailout from itself" (p. 15).

Also connected to the issue of personal distance are subordinate choices involving ethical dilemmas. In *Crimes of Obedience*, authors Kelman and Hamilton (1989) discuss former president Richard Nixon and suggest part of the answer to the Watergate question: why did so many people who had been trained to uphold the law and took oaths to that effect violate those laws in the name of loyalty to a superior?

The authors state that in the Nixon White House, the staff were so close to the centers of power that they identified with the authority structure and were caught up in its glory and mystique. The result was that they tended to exaggerate the president's moral claim on their loyalties. They desperately wished to be liked and included and went to great lengths to avoid risking incurring the displeasure or anger of the top authority.

Liabilities of a Low-Distance Orientation

If you lean toward low distance in your exchanges with your boss and have a more personal orientation, look out for the following:

1. *Spending too much time and energy managing the relationship.* It should not consume consistently large chunks of your time together. When time is short, and there are clear task demands, you may want to leave it out.

2. *The use of personal information by your boss.* If your boss makes any inappropriate comments or uses such information against you, first address the situation as you would any problem. If it continues, it may be wise to withhold some information.

3. *Feeling personally rejected when your ideas are rejected.* Feedback on your performance or ideas should not be taken as personal criticism. Managers with high affiliative needs often feel personally rejected if their ideas are not accepted. Try to keep acceptance of you as a person separate from acceptance of your work, actions, ideas, and proposals. And look out for a reluctance on the part of your boss to give you this important feedback. You need it, and the boss needs to avoid withholding this information from you.

4. *Feeling reluctant to criticize your boss's ideas.* Remember, being too tight with the boss has resulted in more than a few subordinate managers implementing policies they should have questioned and challenged.

5. *The development of a romance or inappropriate intimacies.* The workplace can be an incubator for close relationships. This is particularly true in cross-gender boss-subordinate relationships. Where romantic distractions intrude, that *will* be noticed and become public. It is likely to distract not only those most directly involved, but the entire work group as well. Intimate *developmental* involvement for work and career purposes can be, and should be, separated from inappropriate physical intimacies. If, as a pair, you find yourself unable to manage this, get help from a trustworthy third party.

Too much contact or personal interest can be a problem. But too little can deprive both the boss and the subordinate of information needed for the subordinate's development. It can reduce the quality of working life and quite probably lead to errors in task assignment and performance expectations. For example, the boss, seeing a drop in work performance but lacking knowledge of the subordinate's situation, may make erroneous conclusions about the subordinate manager's motivation. In one situation, an executive reported that a boss, oblivious to his impending divorce, put him on warning for a noticeable drop in performance. The pressure from the boss worsened the executive's performance and nearly caused him to resign.

Liabilities of a High-Distance Orientation

If you lean toward high distance in your exchanges with your boss, and have a more role orientation, look out for the following:

1. *Being left out of the backstage information channels*. We all know that much important and work-relevant exchange happens in informal, out-of-work settings. Too thick a wall between you and your boss may result in your being left out. People may read it as a wish on your part to be separate or may simply lose interest in you as a person.

2. *Losing developmental opportunity*. Your boss may simply not know what excites you or interests you or how you see yourself developing. Even a well-intentioned and genuinely interested boss would find it difficult to know how to assist you, sponsor you, or channel resources to support you unless you make your attitudes quite clear.

3. *Missing out on good assignments*. If your boss is not aware of all your skills, including the less obvious ones, you may not get the choice assignments that call for someone with your talents.

4. *Feeling personally isolated and lacking support*. You may find yourself handling difficulties by yourself when there are good supports all around you. Because people do not know of your needs or concerns, they will not think to offer important assistance, extend understanding, adjust expectations, or just pitch in to help.

5. *Feeling stressed*. We have known for some time that just talking with a sympathetic person (particularly one who, like your boss, has control over resources available to you and demands placed on you) can go a long way to reduce emotional burdens and release energy for other purposes. You may not need to go into extensive detail, but you do have to be willing to let go of some personal information. Personal disclosure can help you lead a healthier work life and reduce stress.

A Matter of Personal Preference?

As we reflect on these different leanings among managers, it is tempting to suggest that this is just a matter of personal preference or style and that people are, well, different.

But, given the inevitability of these effects in organizational functioning, for better and for worse, it makes more sense for boss managers and subordinate managers to handle these feelings and interpersonal processes in ways that can promote work and career effectiveness and improve the quality of work life. This means a more deliberate, less reflexive, management of self and relationships on the dimension of personal distance. You can make choices. Sometimes, for some situations and tasks, a more distant or objective form of relating will be appropriate. For other situations and tasks, a more personal, or close, form of relating will be most effective.

Like it or not, the choice to relate more personally or in a more role-oriented way has consequences and impact on the work of both bosses and subordinate managers. You need to manage your orientation to this aspect of style and adjust it to the circumstances or tasks you and your boss face.

Men and Women at Work

Clarity about the issue of personal distance becomes particularly important in the case of cross-gender authority relationships. The authority relationship is often implicated in the many instances of sexual harassment, discrimination, and, though less discussed, workplace romances. The personal and organizational trauma created by the inept handling of personal distance between bosses and subordinates in the workplace can create significant trauma, both personal and organizational. Cross-gender pairs need to develop a heightened understanding and appreciation of appropriate and inappropriate personal contact.

They also need to pay close attention to the distinction between healthy developmental intimacy and risky and damaging romantic intimacy. Out of a need for self-protection, too many women are forced to retreat from necessary mentoring and developmental relationships because of fears they may be exploited. In most of the reported instances, inappropriate intimacies between (usually) male bosses and female subordinate managers involve the (usually) lower-power woman's being reassigned or even losing her job. For their part, male managers tend to withdraw from these relationships for fear of misunderstandings and worry over how critical feedback will received and responded to. (See Crary, 1987, for an excellent discussion of these issues.) As will be discussed later, higher distance in this relationship can also make influence and conflict resolution more difficult.

Combining Deference and Distance

Although we have, at this point, only two legs (deference and distance) on our three-legged stool (divergence is to come in the next chapter), let us take a look at some ways that our attitude toward power sharing and our attitude toward personal closeness or distance might combine.

Consider, for example, the manager who tends to defer to the boss (high deference), is open to the boss's influence, and is comfortable with receiving direction. It turns out that this manager has a preference for more personal relating in the relationship (low distance). We could characterize this orientation as one of being a friendly helpmate. This subordinate is not likely to do much challenging in the relationship and, depending on the strength of the interpersonal need, would place a great deal of value on positive, harmonious relations. As we begin to vary these preferences somewhat, we see that they form a basis for several of the accommodating subordinate styles, namely the Helper and the Partisan styles.

Or take a different combination. Say a manager is low on deference (is inclined to push for influence with the boss) and is high on distance (is more role oriented). This manager would probably tend to be aggressive and vocal in work relations with the boss and would be unlikely to personalize the relationship, preferring instead to maintain a separateness or independence in the relationship. We can easily imagine the boss, who would have little information about this manager's personal makeup or motivational patterns, wondering about the source of the subordinate's contentiousness. The boss might very well value (or mistrust) this subordinate manager but is likely to stand apart from the relationship as well. In other words, the boss would feel a need to protect himself in the face of such challenge.

The research data clearly show that this combination (low deference and high distance) is associated with poor relationship quality between managers and their bosses. This particular combination appears in the foundation for two of the styles to be discussed in Chapter Five: the Independent and the Gamesman.

But the full and unique character of all these styles comes about when we add the final piece of the puzzle. In Chapter Four, we will look at the last factor, divergence.

Chapter Four

Aligning with and Trusting Your Boss: Degrees of Divergence

It is difficult for me to determine the importance of
goal convergence in my own authority relationships
because I have never been in the situation where my
goals did not coincide with my superior's.
> —*A manager in the research project*

I very rarely see things the same way as others,
particularly bosses, in the organization.
> —*Another manager in the research project*

When you do not understand something your boss is doing, are you inclined to assume you just do not understand the big picture? When this occurs, is it easy for you to simply trust your manager? Do your co-workers think you are naive or a bit of a Pollyanna in your trust for your boss? Do you feel *they* are unnecessarily suspicious of people higher up? Have you been advised by others to be on guard against your bosses? Do you most often accept your boss's goals and methods as legitimate and desirable? Do you consistently avoid political entanglements and resist being recruited into opinion coalitions? Does it make you nervous when co-workers wish to talk with you about their disagreement with the boss?

If you answered yes to some or all of these, or if you lean toward a yes answer, it suggests you have an orientation to low divergence.

When something your boss is doing seems hard to fathom, do

you become concerned with protecting yourself? Do you mistrust your boss with some frequency? Are you often suspicious and trying to find things out about your boss's activities, contacts, communications with others? Do you often feel that you are working at cross-purposes? Do you sense your boss is very concerned about or unhappy with the direction and progress in his own career? Do you believe that your career is of distinctly secondary interest to your boss? Do you sense that your boss keeps you deliberately in the dark on things that are relevant to you, like plans, budgets, or goals? Do you spend time attempting to gauge your peers' level of support for the boss? Do you feel your boss's plans and activities sometimes (or frequently) go against the goals and the interests of the organization? Or the public? Are these things undiscussable?

If you answered yes to some or all of these, or lean toward a yes answer, it suggests you have an orientation to high divergence.

About Divergence

Now that we have described deference and distance, the final piece of our puzzle falls into place when we consider divergence—the extent to which a subordinate manager assumes alignment with the boss's goals. Divergence is not really about whether we *ever* disagree with our bosses; almost everyone does at one time or another. Divergence is much more about a habit or persistent tendency toward agreement or disagreement with our bosses over goals and the methods used to achieve them.

This tendency comes about because managers differ in how much they allow those in positions of authority to define and legitimize goals and methods. Some describe it as the degree of overlap people see between their personal definition of success and the roles and tasks that the boss or the organization asks them to take. It is this underlying difference in how much a manager trusts the boss to set the goals that makes for low or high divergence, not just agreement or disagreement.

Divergence is thus related to a basic dilemma all subordinates face: Do you see the boss, in general, as an ally to be trusted or a competitor to be on guard against? How a subordinate manager resolves this dilemma establishes the basis for cooperative or adversarial tendencies in boss-subordinate relationships.

This basic dilemma may seem to be related to the question of deference. Although deference and divergence are sometimes easy to confuse, they are actually separate factors in the boss-subordinate relationship.

For example, a manager who is quite aligned with the boss where basic goals are concerned (low divergence) might still push hard for influence in decision making (low deference). Just because a subordinate agrees to the same goals as the boss, it does not follow that the subordinate will always defer to the boss's judgment or ideas. As we will see later when we discuss the various style combinations, the Independent style is characterized by low divergence and low deference.

Or take the opposite case, where a manager does not agree with the boss about basic goals but does defer to the boss (high divergence, high deference). You can see that this is quite a different situation, involving the subordinate in perhaps hiding feelings of dissatisfaction with goals behind a mask of deference. We will see this combination later when we consider the Whistleblower style.

The important thing to remember is that divergence (extent of agreement on basic goals) is not the same as deference (extent of pushing for influence). Of course, having said that, I should point out that many managers who agree with the boss also defer to the boss. We will see this is the Military style.

Some readers may still wonder, won't a subordinate manager who disagrees on basic goals eventually push back? In other words, doesn't high divergence eventually lead to low deference? The answer is that this occurs much less often than you might think. These two characteristics are only mildly correlated, especially in men (women show a stronger correlation).

If a manager sees a lot of goal disagreement and feels suspicious of his bosses, attempts to directly influence those bosses *might* result. However, keep in mind that such direct confrontation depends, in a way, on a certain level of trust being present. Making our concerns known to our bosses, stating them clearly, involves a certain vulnerability. Most of us need to feel somewhat safe. We need to feel some measure of trust in order to confront the boss. But a high-divergence manager does not easily trust and so leans toward self-protectiveness.

Rather than trying to directly influence the boss, high-divergence managers would generally choose other options: passive or active sabotage of bosses' directives, quiet "CYA" activity, inactivity (doing nothing), independent action (the subordinate manager does what she thinks should be done), finding allies and forming a coalition, leaving the organization, or blowing the whistle.

Sometimes, too, the high-divergence subordinate manager gives in and goes along with the boss. In spite of misgivings, the subordinate manager will do what is asked, often to his regret. In these instances, he attempts to blunt his attention to the question of divergence; he will shrug and sigh, "The boss is the boss."

Overview of Low Divergence

Low-divergence managers tend to accept the basic premises within which they work. Donna's statement describes some of the main features of this orientation.

> I tend toward goal convergence. I feel comfortable with this style because I believe that subordinates should share the goals of the organization. Because if I don't, why am I here? I don't have a problem with my superior taking an interest in one of my projects. There are times when this is helpful and can lead to an earlier completion date on the project.
>
> I see that the potential liability is being seen as a meek follower. But in my current organization, this is not necessarily a bad thing.

There is one ultimate goal, patient care, and you are ostracized if you are not seen as a team player.

Low-divergence managers like Donna tend to see the boss as an ally, not a competitor. They are prone to assume that the boss's interests are pretty much their own interests and vice versa. They generally assume, even when they cannot clearly determine what goals their work is serving, that they are in alignment with the organization and address the organization's legitimate interests. They tend to believe that the boss is concerned in a balanced way with their career and general well-being.

Many low-divergence subordinates see the big decisions being made at higher organizational levels and accept that their primary contributions are made by joining with others to operationalize decisions. Low-divergence subordinates may, or may not, be deferential on matters that they feel fall within the scope of their role. They may push their bosses aggressively for influence in many things, such as decisions about methods, how to operationalize goals, assignments, role definitions, access to developmental opportunities, and so on. But they assume, at the same time, that they and the boss share fundamental goals.

Subordinates like Donna are often seen as team players, valuable, reliable, hard-working staff. Many low-divergence managers say that this orientation involves much less stress at work. Very little energy is devoted to questioning the goals of the group or organization. Such a posture can also help the managers get continuing support from their bosses and help to maintain a steady stream of information as well.

Getting Along and Going Along

Underlying this orientation are several common values. To some low-divergence subordinates, accepting the goals and methods of the organization and the boss is synonymous with accepting membership in the organization. Many organizations promote this equation. Government agencies, hospitals and other health care organizations, the military, and business organizations rank lowest in divergence; the highest are universities and social service organizations.

For these managers, low divergence is equated with loyalty to the boss, to their function, and to the larger organization. Loyalty is a personal value, and they want to belong and be seen as team players.

Others with this orientation express confidence in and respect the expertise of their bosses. They figure the boss is the boss for a reason. Some, like the engineering program manager below, use their divergence orientation to purchase independence from authority. They make certain their support for established goals is recognized and then ask, in effect, to be left alone by their bosses.

> Usually, I view authority in nonadversarial terms, because I espouse the goals of my organization as my own. I do not try to subvert authority, but I also do not encourage a very close involvement of authority with my day-to-day work.

Some younger managers adopt this orientation for purposes of learning and modeling themselves after their boss, who is often an example of organizational success.

> My divergence rating, which leans toward goal convergence, was a function of my desire to survive in this new world. My boss's goals were my goals due to my inexperience and naiveté.

Others with a low-divergence orientation express a discomfort with the "big" questions, those that consider larger functional or organizational goals and purposes. They are not inclined to raise questions about the larger purposes or ends of their work. They sometimes comment that they dislike stress, conflict, or ambiguous problems.

Divergence *is* associated with level of educational achievement. Managers with a bachelor's degree or less tend to be more convergent, perhaps to gain the necessary sponsorship of higher-level managers. They often indicate they find it difficult to conceptualize the organization in its larger environmental context. Besides feeling they do not have the expertise, low-divergence managers also indicate they do not have the mandate or the role to question basic goals. Managers at the master's level and above tend to be more divergent, perhaps because they possess both the conceptual skills and occupy the sorts of roles that support divergent thinking.

Low-divergence managers show some varying forms common to several of the styles. Managers using the Military style, for example, accept organizational goals and are generally accommodating to their bosses, generally assuming that their bosses are acting consistent with, and in support of, larger, legitimate systems goals. When this is not clear, managers with the Military style tend to discount their own understanding and just assume all is as it should be. They assume that the vantage point of their role simply prevents them from appreciating the necessity for their activities.

Partisan style managers, on the other hand, are more zealous and energetically assimilate the boss's goals as their own. Devotion and loyalty here tend to be attached to the boss, with the organization itself less in focus. The Partisan goes beyond the Military style in replacing obedience and accommodation with zeal and in attaching more to the boss than to the organization. The Helper tends to avoid goal questions altogether in order to maintain harmonious relations with the boss. Low divergence is the path of least resistance. It is strongly connected to lower levels of boss-subordinate conflict and less troubled (though not necessarily more effective) relationships.

Low-divergence managers are not necessarily accommodating or compliant if their divergence orientation is coupled with a low-deference orientation, as in the Independent style. This style generally accepts organizational goals but feels undersupported by the bosses and not particularly trusting of them. Independent managers, as the name implies, will energetically resist intrusion by the boss into what they feel is their task domain. While they accept overall goals, they want the rest to be left to their discretion.

From the standpoint of organizational functions, managers with a low-divergence orientation tend to be found in accounting, production and operations, engineering, quality control, and human resources. Those with a high-divergence orientation are often found in sales and marketing, and research and development. It seems to make some sense that managers in those functions concerned with supporting the status quo—success within current mission definition—would be more oriented to low divergence. Those charged with getting the organization to respond more to the external environment or moving the organization into new activities would be less so.

Advantages of Low Divergence

If you are beginning to see yourself in this description of low divergence, what benefits can you expect to bring to your relationship with the boss and to your organization?

- You will make a good team player who is able to take on the goals of the organization as his or her own. Your boss will likely appreciate the way you leave questions about larger systems goals and priorities to those who have the mandate, the information, and, presumably, the training to deal with them.

- You and your boss are likely to have an agreeable relationship with minimal conflict that can be easily contained and managed. You will have a much better relationship with the boss than managers who have a high-divergence orientation.

- Your orientation is likely to enhance communication with your boss, and information exchange will be high.

- You are likely to receive preferential treatment in assignments, since many boss managers are reluctant to give assignments to subordinate managers who express and hold onto divergent views.

- Should you desire it, you are likely to gain a measure of operating independence since the boss will (in general) be confident of the goals you are pursuing. He or she will be less concerned with monitoring your activities.

- Your career prospects are likely to be better, with more fluid progression. Higher-level managers tend to promote into their midst lower-level managers who support the current goal structure.

Overview of High Divergence

Remember that divergence is related to the basic subordinate dilemma of whether or not to trust the boss. We have seen how managers with the low-divergence orientation tend to trust the boss and work within a framework of goal alignment. Other managers, however, tend toward being wary and watchful of the boss. This is the hallmark of the high-divergence orientation. High-divergence managers feel that the boss is not an ally and may even be a competitor, and that their own methods and goals are in conflict with the boss's.

Remember, too, that this orientation is not about whether you *ever* disagree with your boss. Rather, it asks the question "Is there a tendency to *usually* or habitually see things differently and disagree with your bosses over where you are going?"

There appear to be three facets to high divergence.

1. Managers whose orientation to high divergence comes about through chronic conflicts over goals and mission; this could describe the Whistleblower style.

2. Those who basically accept goals but struggle over method, procedures, the ways to achieve them; an example is the Rebel style.

3. Those who accept both goals and methods but feel their bosses are not allies, that they must be continuously on guard and self-protective; they are generally less high on the divergence scale.

As is the case with all the other orientations, managers who adopt a high-divergence orientation have a sensible logic that supports their leaning.

Russell, a project financial manager in the computer industry, voices a simple conviction that guides his interactions with his bosses.

> [I have] uncomfortable feelings around my boss's lack of communications regarding his organizational plans. . . . The behavior of those in authority needs to be open to scrutiny and be scrutinized.

To managers like Russell, a high-divergence orientation is just sensible. Such managers tend to see organizations in Darwinian terms. Their favorite metaphor for the organization is a jungle where upper-level managers will take credit that should go to their subordinate managers. In this view, boss managers will also lay on subordinate managers blame that they should assume for themselves. These subordinate managers can, and often do, point to numerous experiences, both direct and indirect, of the abuse of power by people in authority. Perhaps partly because of their personal histories and early experiences, their struggles with people in authority can take on symbolic meaning and become quite escalated.

Political maneuvering can displace task energy as these high-divergence managers become self-protective. This is particularly true where organizational decision making has become politicized, organizational goals are in flux, or the organization is undergoing redesign or retrenchment. When there are no clear, public, well-communicated goals for the organization, high-divergence managers will assume a defensive, and sometimes an offensive, attitude. It is also worth mentioning that high-divergence managers seem to find it easier to maintain and assert their sense of uniqueness and individuality through this orientation.

Other high-divergence managers have histories of involvement in organizational change and commonly occupy roles that involve organizational change. Sometimes these are formally designated as change roles, sometimes not: the emphasis on change may have come about through the manager having had numerous new project assignments. Michael, one of these managers, and the manager who made the statement mentioned at the beginning of this chapter ("I very rarely see things the same way as others in the organization") went on to say:

> I believe there are better and more efficient ways to accomplish the tasks which must be completed and am not afraid to cross "boundaries" when I recognize something is not efficient or just. The organization I work for is very political and there are few within the management staff who know how to play the political game. I have mastered the ability to work with anyone, which has given me the utmost advantage. I continually monitor the thoughts and attitudes of all the managers.

Most of Michael's work has involved organizational change, and he is often called upon to struggle with the status quo. His work supports and is even synergistic with his personal orientation. He scores very high on divergence—in the ninety-ninth percentile in fact.

Besides the philosophical conviction of many high-divergence managers and the explanations involving the management of change, managers with high-divergence orientations are often well-educated specialists who probably do know more about problems within their expertise than their bosses do.

Jan, an executive in the auto industry, is an example. She is high on divergence and she feels that her independent orientation is necessary for her to do her job. Most often, she views her bosses as obstacles. She is, however, aware of some liabilities and risks.

> I tend to see my relationship with authority in adversarial terms. I do feel that most superiors do not consider subordinates' needs or concerns in decision making and I do feel that I see things very differently than those in authority. . . . I feel that [my boss] puts me in a position to make all his decisions and then he criticizes any conclusions I come to, but he never suggests any alternatives. I also feel that most times he does not know what he is talking about when he is making those criticisms, and I get very annoyed.
>
> I rarely ask his opinion on anything, partly because I always have to answer at least ten questions for him first, and partly because I do not like to ask for help in the first place. Of course, I disagree with most of what he says and since I never get specific direction anyway, after such encounters I usually leave his office and head straight for the aspirin bottle. I also usually go ahead and do what I had originally intended to do in the first place.

Jan admits her comments describe her relationship with most of her bosses. Her orientation to divergence has certain advantages. She is alert to her own self-interests and is quick to see choices and decisions by her bosses in a larger context. With this orientation, subordinate managers are likely to spot dangers early and be able to act promptly to defend their own interests or the interests of others who may be harmed.

It is also in the nature of organizational systems that higher-level directives and policies often fail to adequately consider implementation issues and problems. What may be an elegant solution to a problem may simply be undoable at the operating level. Middle ranks of managers are usually the ones who have to reconcile these demands. This can easily lead middle managers to wonder why certain decisions were taken or to feel that they are being given impossible tasks. Such stresses can easily lead more divergent managers to promptly move to their own defense.

Remember that a high-divergence orientation is not necessarily a problem for the organization, though it does usually lead to stressed boss-subordinate relationships. Where the high-divergence manager is involved in managing change, or operates from an independent work design, or is a technical specialist, such an orientation becomes a plus.

As managers progress higher in the organization, the research shows, they become less divergent in their thinking and buy in more to prevailing goals, methods, and approaches. This is true whether they start off as high-divergence managers or as low-divergence ones. Over time, the organization exerts a press toward a sort of conformity.

It is not clear whether the managers that rise in the organization become better informed as they have access to more critical information and priorities, have been co-opted in their thinking (as the price for entry to higher levels), or have simply become the ones who decide on the current goals, methods, and approaches, and thus support them. In any case, there tends to be a tension between higher- and lower-level managers around this issue. Lower-level managers tend to be more divergent, though apparently as they progress upward they see less and less reason to be so. This draws our attention to an important organizational dilemma.

The managers who are most likely to engage in innovative and transformative thinking about organizational mission, goals, and methods are the least likely to have the power to do anything about it (given traditional structures). They are most often found in the lower levels of management or in less powerful staff positions. When a manager obtains the power, chances are the price has been buying into the prevailing view of organizational purposes and goals.[1]

This research finding—that higher level equals less divergence—lends additional support to the necessity of creating, within traditional structures, reservations for innovation that are given access to the top authorities of the organization. This top group should not, however, be only top management, but rather should emphasize proactive directors and outside advisers.

Advantages of High Divergence

If you see yourself leaning toward high divergence, what benefits might you bring to the boss-subordinate relationship and to your organization?

- You are likely to be adept at placing decisions into a larger context, asking the difficult questions, and challenging your organization to think about, or rethink, its purposes and values.
- You are likely to be sensitive to ethical dilemmas and contradictions between organizational pronouncements and behavior.
- You may be able to spot dangers early and help your organization avoid making mistakes.
- You can help your organization focus its attention on how it is accomplishing its work, and you are not reluctant to promote new, perhaps even radical approaches.
- Because you have high technical skills, your high-divergence orientation will help your boss and organization to improve decision making and effectiveness.
- Your vigilant nature will help you be sensitive and responsive to genuine threats to your career, other self-interests, and the interests of your peers.

The Flip Side: Disadvantages

As we have seen, both low and high divergence have distinct advantages. Both orientations, when pushed to the extreme, also have severe disadvantages.

The powerful advantages of low divergence, which so often create the team spirit so prized in organizations, are countered by some serious disadvantages. If the subordinate manager does not develop and maintain a sensitivity to divergent interests, she might find herself pursuing unethical, immoral, or dangerous courses of action, courses that might harm her, others in the organization, or the organization itself. When pushed too far, the low-divergence orientation can result in a sort of passive collusion—the negative side of agreement and cooperation. This is dangerous when goals are ambiguous or unclear or when those in authority are engaged in mainly self-oriented activities. One low-divergence manager remarked, quite accurately, "I can often be taken in by a superior's charismatic presentation and not be aware of his faults." Also, managers with this orientation may not be developing broader conceptual skills that would help them be effective at higher levels.

Managerial Confluence: Going Along

Since low-divergence managers are slow to recognize diverging interests and reluctant to engage in conflict with their bosses, they are also slow to defend themselves, their organizations, or the larger community. In the presence of goal conflict, such managers may even become immobilized. They may also not have developed the necessary political skills and alliances to help resolve these kinds of issues. This sort of innocence, dislike for ambiguity, or lack of awareness about implications becomes a blindness to the effects of the manager's actions in a larger context.

The result can be an unwitting helpfulness in amplifying the effects of bad leadership decisions through the instrument of their organization. History has repeatedly shown us the horrors that become possible when dangerous, unjust, or ridiculous policies are made real, amplified, and extended through the vast reach of organizational instruments.

It has been suggested that such a process can be called "authorization." This happens when organizational authority explicitly sanctions or implicitly condones acts that are usually unacceptable but become acceptable in the organization because they are approved by or appear to be acceptable to those higher up and a subordinate manager feels powerless to resist. This authorization becomes a self-sustaining force and allows, even encourages, continuation of the actions. Authorization relieves organizational participants from the necessity of making moral decisions or being confronted with the immorality of their actions. Kelman and Hamilton, in *Crimes of Obedience* (1989), suggest that "for bureaucratic actors, authorization may override normal moral considerations either by elevating loyalty to leader or organization to the highest obligation or by invoking a transcendent mission" (p. 29).

In this process, leadership removes (or, perhaps more accurately, distracts) those in subordinate roles from normal considerations of divergent interests and goals by creating, or stipulating, a transcendent goal, priority, or principle.

A tragic instance of this can be seen in the behavior of the engineers at Morton-Thiokol and NASA, who took the largest share of the blame for the explosion of the *Challenger* shuttle. After the accident, they testified that they complained, sent memos to their bosses, and (carefully) protested that they "could not recommend a launch" on that cold morning. But, as was pointed out later by their superiors, they (the engineers) did not recommend *against* a launch. The engineers defended themselves by saying that they saw themselves as loyal employees who believed in the chain of command and accepted its decisions. Ben Powers of NASA stated, "You don't override your chain of command. My boss was there; I made my position known to him; he did not choose to pursue it. At that point it's up to him; he doesn't have to give me any reasons; he doesn't work for me; it's his prerogative" (Mainero and Tromley, 1989, p. 306).

Once disagreement, divergent thinking, and even diversity are removed or suppressed, dialogue is destroyed. If organizational machinery and personal managerial preferences defeat attention to larger goals being served and the ramifications of our actions, no one feels responsible. Other courses of action or belief wither, and no other course seems plausible or, for many, desirable. The extremes of low divergence can thus be quite dangerous.

Managerial Contentiousness: Going Political

At the same time, a high-divergence orientation, for all its benefits, if pushed too far, can have negative results as well. Managers with exaggerated high divergence, if positioned well or if skilled in backstage maneuvers, can bring about a sort of organizational paralysis. Even if not paralysis, a grievous wasting of energies while coping with politics diverts people from doing their jobs.

Where goals are not clear, known, understood, or accepted, organizational decision making can fall captive to political processes where choices and actions are selected based on who has what power, not on careful analysis of what best fulfills a balanced and accepted mission. This can lead to a weakened concentration and coordination of organizational resources on achieving worthwhile objectives. Where divergence is very high and very widespread, the organization becomes a chessboard, a jungle, or a battlefield.

When those who are concerned with self-protection build sufficiently large followings, it is hard to concentrate on the primary tasks of the organization. Ineffective dispersal of energies and a loss of focus are the results. Speaking in a larger social context, Warren Bennis, the noted leadership theorist, once commented on the consequences of a widespread refusal to accommodate legitimate authority. He observed that there had grown up a counterauthority trend in society that represented a serious threat to focused and coordinated action. He went on to say that this trend leads to a fragmentation that exists more or less in all organizations and "marks the end not only of community, a sense of shared values and symbols, but of consensus, an agreement reached despite differences. These pressure groups are intentionally fragmented . . . going their separate and often conflicting ways. . . . So what we have now is a new form of politics. . . . It is the politics of multiple advocacies. They represent people who are fed up with being ignored, neglected, excluded, denied, subordinated" (Bennis, 1976a, p. 5).

Another negative result occurs in the boss-subordinate relationship itself. The high-divergence orientation acts as a corrosive in the relationship and is likely to defeat any possible synergies, whether they are for the subordinate manager's development or the accomplishment of work.

Divergence and Relationship Quality and Effectiveness

The divergence scale is a powerful indicator of difficulties in the boss-subordinate relationship. There is also some connection between the other two factors and quality of relationships. For example, as deference increases, the relationship tends to improve slightly. Likewise, as distance increases, the relationship becomes a little worse. However, where divergence is concerned, these slight effects become positive, strong, and significant.

As divergence increases and the subordinate is more prone to see goal separation, the quality of the relationship deteriorates in close proportion. As the subordinate manager increases in seeing divergent goals and interests, it is very likely that he or she will get along increasingly poorly with authority and will feel (and probably be) less effective in the relationship.[2] The association between divergence and relationship quality recommends that particularly careful self-management by the subordinate is called for or the relationship can become quite stressed and tattered. This issue should be the subject of ongoing dialogue between levels of management.

This finding also suggests that when there are problems in the boss-subordinate relationship, the *first* matter to take up is their respective interpretations of the goals they serve and the methods that best achieve those goals.

Chapter Five

Getting a True Picture
of Yourself:
Matters of Style

I am definitely the rebel. My bosses can hardly finish
a sentence before I blurt out, "I disagree!" Sometimes
I don't even let them finish. I just think I usually
have a better way to get things done—I think my
antics amuse them . . . at least sometimes.

—An executive in the research project

I can see that my style is more of the accommodating
type—a good soldier. It . . . probably has a lot to do
with my upbringing, my years in the service, and my
tendency to go along with my bosses. I assume they
have the bigger picture and will try to look out for
me and my interests.

—Another executive in the research project

The three factors in a subordinate manager's orientation toward
authority—deference, distance, and divergence—could theoretically be combined in many different ways. In practice, however, it
turns out there are nine ways that the factors commonly combine
to create common subordinate styles. In this chapter I describe and
discuss each of these nine styles.

Up to this point, we have talked of the three orientations in
terms of high and low versions. In reality, as you might expect, managers are not always either high or low. In this chapter, therefore,
we will speak of the in-between degrees of orientation, including

medium, medium high, medium low, very high, very low, and so forth. These descriptions refer to numerical scores on the diagnostic instrument I used to measure the orientations (see the Appendix). These style descriptions were the result of an extensive analysis process that uncovered a number of useful strategies employed by managers in dealing with their bosses. The very high and very low descriptions tend toward the extreme orientations, which as we have seen are sometimes related to the disadvantages of the various orientations.

Let us begin with an overview of all nine styles. Remember, the styles fit into three supercategories:

1. The *accommodating styles* are those in which the subordinate manager works as a supportive assistant to those in authority within the structure provided. These include the Military style, the Helper, the Diplomat, and the Partisan.
2. The *autonomous styles* are those in which the subordinate manager works apart from, or avoids, authority, preferring to create his or her own structure within broad guidelines. These include the Independent style and the Counselor style.
3. The *adversarial styles* are those in which the subordinate manager works in opposition to authority, resisting or even breaking down structure. These include the Gamesman, the Rebel, and the Whistleblower.

Each group of styles has its uses and supports its managers and their organization in different ways:

- The accommodating styles support through cooperative enactment or implementation of managerial directives. With varying degrees of enthusiasm, they will align themselves and make it all happen (generally) as their bosses wish.
- The autonomous styles support through more self-guided achievement of overall goals. They value a more loosely

coupled way of operating. Outside of some general goals, they prefer self-management to being directed, loose consultation arrangements to being monitored. They are particularly useful in change activities.

- The adversarial styles support through confrontation (though many of their bosses might say it does not feel like support). These styles are more "in your face" when it comes to authority relationships. Whether the more obstreperous Rebel, the strategic Gamesman, or the quietly assertive Whistleblower, adversarial managers alert their bosses and organizations to alternative ways of operating and basic values choices that could otherwise be overlooked or ignored, to the organization's detriment.

Demographics of the Study

Another factor that I have not discussed much up to this point is the prevalence of certain styles in certain types of organizations or in certain functions within an organization. This aspect of style will become a part of the discussion in this chapter. For example, the accommodating styles appear more frequently than the autonomous or adversarial styles in business and government organizations (which has implications for innovation and creativity). The autonomous and adversarial styles appear more frequently in educational institutions (and that has implications for their leaders' prospects in developing consensus and narrowing their strategic focus in times of shrinking resources).

Please bear in mind that such descriptors tell only in a general way about the style. To say a certain style is more often found in a certain place does not mean that is the only place it is found. In other words, all types are found in all functions and organizations. It is just that managers using certain styles tend to self-select into, and stay in, functions that support and reward their style of operating with people in authority. Further, all the descriptors within a style description may not apply equally to all those who are members of that group. The more a manager's ratings approach the "ideal" for that style, the more things are likely to apply. When they are further away from the ideal (but still a member of that group), fewer attributes will apply.

Of particular relevance here is the fact that the population I studied was almost exclusively American and Caucasian. Two-thirds of the participants were men and one-third women; average age was thirty-nine; and most were well educated (85 percent had a bachelor's degree or better). Slightly more than half (55 percent) came from business organizations; the rest were from health care, education, government, or the military. Roughly 60 percent were in middle or upper management.

The Accommodating Styles

Accommodating subordinates tend to be high on deference and low on divergence. Their orientation to authority is, overall, one of agreeableness and accommodation. They have little need to influence the boss, and they display a comfort in, and even a zeal for, the implementer role. When concerted action is the goal, accommodating subordinates are a real asset.

Unless they receive focused skills training, these are not likely candidates for genuine participatory management, since they prefer structure and direction. They generally experience the absence of structure and direction not as freedom or discretion or empowerment but rather as a sort of formlessness or even chaos. In most cases, they value a role-oriented relationship and readily accept the boss's goals as legitimate, or at least acceptable. They tend to believe that people in authority are well informed and generally right in the courses of action they pursue.

When there is disagreement, accommodating subordinates are likely to discount their own views or surrender to the belief that making decisions is the boss's prerogative (and responsibility). In discounting their own views, such subordinates are prone to believe they have insufficient expertise, are missing the big picture, or that their information is incomplete or ambiguous. When confronted with obstructions, accommodating subordinates will make efforts to overcome them and, if failing, will return to the boss for further instructions and assistance.

Now let us look at each accommodating style in detail.

Military (high deference, high distance, low divergence)

This is one of the most prevalent styles in the business world. High deference means that a subordinate manager with this style will not often push for influence. High distance means the relationship with authority is role oriented—friendly but impersonal. Low divergence means the subordinate manager assumes goal compatibility and harmony; trust and loyalty are high priorities.

This is a common male profile, and, as the name implies, this subordinate manager prizes being reliable, taking orders well, and playing the implementer role. While generally distributed throughout all the organizational functions, this type tends to be made up of older, midlevel line managers without strong educational backgrounds (bachelor's degree or less in most cases). As such, they tend to be less organizationally secure and are likely to value loyalty and obedience over initiative, creativity, and discretion (in themselves and in others).

They are sensitive to signs of status differentiations, but as long as the boss does not adopt numerous trappings of higher status, they will be satisfied with their lower position. They may like to be asked for their input but are not bothered overmuch if the boss's decisions do not reflect their views. They prefer to be seen as the loyal citizens and team players and want to avoid sticking their necks out.

Although the accommodating styles are generally low on divergence, which implies overall trust for the boss, for the Military style, the trust is somewhat qualified. While there is general agreement or acceptance on methods and goals, managers with the Military style do not generally feel that the boss cares much about them as people. They tend not to see the boss as an ally and because of this are inclined to be self-protective and risk averse. These tendencies further support their reluctance about being empowered.

Helper (medium deference, low distance, very low divergence)

This style is common among human resource managers. Medium deference means that a subordinate manager with this style wants influence but will not often push hard for it, fearing the risks in doing so. Unlike many of the low-deference styles, this one does not want to risk the conflict or alienation that sometimes accompanies being more aggressively inner-directed. Low distance means that subordinates with this style will want to have a personal relationship with the boss, emphasizing closeness and personal disclosure. Very low divergence means that these managers will be virtually dependent on the boss to set the general direction and goals under which they work. Helpers tend to be uncomfortable with and avoid the more contentious aspects of organizational politics. They value more harmonious team-oriented activities. They prefer consensus over power and dialogue over argument as a means of accomplishing tasks.

Helpers tend to be younger staff people with college education but few advanced degrees. Although they prefer to have influence, they need to be invited to join in providing input. If they are denied in this, they will satisfy themselves with the role of implementing decisions made by the boss. This medium level of deference comes from their ideology about democratic principles in organizations and not so much from a strong sense of their own expertise. They tend to believe that a subordinate should have influence simply because it is the right way to do things. Their desire for influence thus does not arise from a conviction that they bring unique and important expertise to the table. They are more likely to base their expertise in fostering cooperative relationships.

Helpers want to have a personal relationship with the boss while deemphasizing, or in some cases choosing not to see, the role aspects of boss-subordinate relationships. They are comfortable in self-disclosure and like the boss to express an interest in them as people. Helpers are generally open and easy to get along with. However, their personal preference does not extend to having the boss disclose more personal aspects of his or her own life.

This makes sense when we consider that the Helper also indicates a preference toward charismatic, even aloof bosses. In a low-distance cluster, it is a bit surprising, and counter to what we might expect, that such a preference should appear. However, on closer examination, it appears that the Helper's preference reflects a wish for closer, more personal contact with a more heroic and personally distant figure who can (ideally) provide safety, acceptance, and nurturing. This echoes a parental figure (at least while one is very young)—both personal and aloof in the sense of being all powerful. This suggests that the Helper has less interest in seeing the quirks, foibles, insecurities, and doubts of the boss and more interest in feeling known by, accepted by, and probably sheltered by him.

Helpers see their role as that of a trusting helpmate, an orientation prized by many bosses. They can be quite valuable in emphasizing points of agreement and fostering cooperative work relationships. Their internal gyroscope seems quite fixed on finding win-win solutions when problems arise. This generally valuable skill (particularly in today's team-oriented organizational cultures) can lead them to be conflict averse, almost refusing to see any differences between their needs and goals and those of the boss. In the wrong situation, the strong feeling that the boss is an ally can lead some Helpers into a naive confluence, going along with things that should be opposed. In this, their agreeableness to the goal structure and emphasis on harmonious relations with the boss (normally positive traits) take on a sort of gauzy blindness or an insensitivity to wrong courses of action and conflicts of interest.

Diplomat (high deference, medium distance, medium-high divergence)

The Diplomat style is something like the Military style, except that, being younger, the Diplomat has less trust for the boss and finds more areas of disagreement. Thus high deference—very little push for influence—is combined with medium distance and medium-high divergence. This means that personal contact with the boss is sought, but with caution, because of the Diplomat's uncertainty about whether the boss is an ally or adversary.

Diplomats are most often found in business organizations and usually in marketing, sales, and production. They tend to be well-educated newcomers to the management ranks. Their focus is on learning the rules and being conscientious—at least in being seen that way. Although they want to provide input prior to decision making and carry a stronger sense of their own expertise than the Military style, they do not believe that the boss has any obligation to consult with subordinates before making a decision. A decisive boss who is not overbearing is likely to engender a sense of security in these subordinates. They are comfortable with status distinctions and visible symbols of the status and power differences between themselves and the boss.

Diplomats are guarded in personal relationships to the boss, but offer enough work-related personal disclosure to support development and demonstrate belonging and trust. They are not likely to offer in-depth personal disclosure, because this might make them vulnerable. Though ambivalent and tentative, they are able to see the boss as an ally, sometimes even as a sponsor. Yet the boss can also be something of a foil for the Diplomat. Given the deferential attitude of this subordinate, when there are disagreements, the Diplomat does not opt for direct influencing of the boss but rather artful maneuvering and tactful positioning.

Partisan (very high deference, medium distance, very low divergence)

The Partisan is a more extreme version of the Military style. Where the Military style is high on deference, the Partisan is very high, and where the Military style is low on divergence, the Partisan is very low. Partisan subordinates feel that their overriding obligation is to the boss, not necessarily to their organization; when the boss's goals and those of the organization diverge, the Partisan will be more committed to the goals of the boss.

Partisans are often older males with a lot of seniority in the organization. They tend to be upper-level managers, many in finance and accounting. Even though they tend to have high educational achievements, this does not lead them to insist on voice in decision making. Instead, Partisans are extremely effective implementers, applying considerable ingenuity to making the things desired by their bosses happen. They are fervent, devoted, and biased cheerleaders for the boss. Their job is to support and implement—period. They neither want nor expect to be consulted. In some ways it is the Partisan that is actually being portrayed in stereotypes of the gung-ho soldier. Where the Military style brings conscientious and careful obedience or acquiescence, the Partisan brings commitment and zeal.

Their medium distance score reflects their view of boss as a hero. Partisans want a boss who is accessible and available to them, not aloof or distant, but at the same time they do not look for closeness. They thus want the boss to take a personal interest in them, but they have little wish to reciprocate. This idealization of the boss also means that they are unlikely to be very personally open with the boss or want the boss to be open with them, as this might reveal anxieties and insecurities that would threaten their ideal image of the boss and possibly disrupt any relationship built on such high deference and low divergence. For the Partisan, the boss-subordinate relationship is somewhat like the traditional ideal of a father-son relationship, characterized by (one-sided) respect and idealization.

The Autonomous Styles

The common characteristic uniting all autonomous subordinates is low deference. The subordinate managers in these styles will push for influence in the decision process with their bosses and will see significant need to be careful and self-protective around their bosses. They are not always mistrustful but are alert, watchful, and wary. Their preference is to support authority through independent action and autonomous spheres of operation, preferring to create their own structure rather than have it imposed.

They prefer to be given general directions and decision guidelines and do not like being closely monitored. They will often require some clear understanding about what circumstances will trigger monitoring by the boss and what circumstances will trigger their consultation with the boss. Though accepting of an overall direction, these managers jealously guard their discretion once they are set into motion. Attempts by the boss to intrude will be met with strong resistance.

Women managers are strongly represented in the autonomous styles. They appear in these styles in much higher frequency than predicted by their number in the overall population. Since women also score significantly less deferential than men do (they push more for influence with their bosses), it seems reasonable to suggest that women are more prone to establish themselves as autonomous in their relationships with their bosses.

Independent (low deference, high distance, medium-low divergence)

Independent subordinate managers push for influence with the boss for both ideological and practical reasons; they believe they should be consulted because it is right and because they have needed expertise. Consistent with this, Independents have a strong negative response to status distinctions between a boss and a subordinate. The only meaningful distinctions, in their view, revolve around expertise and access—to information, to prerogatives, to tools to direct action, to levers of power, and to authority.

They are not comfortable with the implementer role and will react negatively, even to the point of resistance, if decisions do not reflect their input. As the name implies, this is a self-directed subordinate. Once agreed upon instructions are given, this subordinate can be hard to influence and is likely to see inquiries and monitoring as intrusion.

In this group, there is a high frequency of relatively young, female middle managers. They are, overall, highly educated but the group is somewhat bipolar, with another large cluster at the lower end of the educational spectrum (less than bachelor's degree).

The Independent's high distance reflects a comfort with and preference for role relating that is guided by the boss's need to know. They provide only necessary role-related disclosure, and sometimes not enough of this. They are not as absolute in their personal reticence as some other high-distance styles, since they do admit to some value in letting the boss know who they are as a person. Even so, Independents are most comfortable working in relative isolation and at a distance, and tend to withhold both personal and task-related information, which can leave the boss in the dark about their activities, intentions, uncertainties, and difficulties.

They are self-protective when struggling with the boss and are likely to take tough and principled stands in disagreements. The boss may view their tough stance as rigidity, because they do not see the boss as an ally and will resist disclosing uncertainty (a real liability when gaps in their knowledge have task consequences). Their divergence score coupled with their high distance score means that in conflict with the boss there is little personal connection to soften or cushion their differences, to provide an underlying connection during struggle.

The Independent generally feels unsupported and will tend to transform differences into escalated, ideological conflicts. Any attempt by a boss to control this type of subordinate manager will validate the Independent's fears and legitimize further evasion or escalation.

Counselor (low deference, very low distance, medium divergence)

Counselors are managerial subordinates with a strong sense of themselves as experts; they reject the implementer role and generally strive to reduce power differences to a razor-thin margin.

Women are disproportionately represented in the Counselor group, which tends to include older staff managers who are very well educated, with well over half holding advanced degrees. They tend to be found less frequently (but are not rare) in business and are more frequently found in education, health care, social service, and consulting organizations.

The Counselor insists on having a voice *and* very much resents status distinctions. Further, unlike some subordinates who like to be consulted but are not concerned if the decision by their bosses does not reflect their input, Counselors will insist that decisions reflect their input. They can be characterized as being quite sensitive to how they are dealt with by their bosses.

Counselors have a strong commitment to personal interaction for better quality of work life and job effectiveness. They seek full personal exchange and expect the boss to reciprocate. The Counselor seeks to place the relationship on a solid interpersonal footing and is likely to resist a relationship in which the boss prefers a more distant orientation. The bosses of such managers can expect occasional reminders that, regardless of organizational level, the managers are "just like everyone one." For Counselors, such personal contact complements and supports effective work and helps to balance feelings of vulnerability. They are likely to pursue work-related disclosure from the boss, including information about the boss's aspirations, ambitions, concerns, motivations, frustrations, and values. They also believe that nonwork information about such things as home life, interests, hobbies, and the struggle for balance has a bearing on work and might give clues to the boss's makeup and thought processes that will make them both more effective.

While they see a significant amount of difference in goals, methods, and procedures with their bosses, Counselors also sense their boss's support and interest. More so than the other styles, Counselors have more of an issues orientation when it comes to divergence, seeing divergence on some issues and convergence on others. They tend to avoid generalizing on the issue of trust and are more oriented to complexly viewing their bosses.

Counselors' very low personal distance eases conflict, because the boss is seen as an ally, and because their personal connection works to keep differences from spilling over into a more mistrustful and antagonistic relationship. Counselors are among the most positive groups in their assessments of relationship quality with their bosses.

The Adversarial Styles

The adversarial group of subordinate managers is *generally* characterized by low deference and high divergence. Managers in the adversarial styles tend to be well educated, and their grounding in their expertise supports their low-deference orientation. They exhibit as strong (or stronger) loyalties to the tenets and codes of their professional disciplines as they do to their organizations. When the requirements of their roles and organizations are placed in conflict with their profession's tenets, professional expertise, or ethics, they are likely to push back in a variety of ways.

The other characteristic that unites these styles is an orientation to high or very high divergence. In general, these subordinates tend to see their bosses as adversaries or competitors, not as allies.

In addition, they tend to disagree a great deal over goals, methods, and procedures, though not in the same ways.

While stressful for their bosses, and sometimes for their organizations, these subordinates do offer important corrective support through challenge and confrontation. However, they pay a price. These styles report more troubled relationships with the boss than any of the other styles; 88 percent of the Gamesmen, 60 percent of the Whistleblowers, and 59 percent of the Rebels report their boss relationships as troubled (compared to 12 to 26 percent for the accommodating styles).

My research found that a majority of managers of all types tended to assess their boss relationships as more positive than they were. However, it appears the adversarial styles make the largest error in underestimating the negative impact of their behavior on their relationships with their bosses. Because of this combination of factors, bosses with high control needs will have a great deal of trouble with these three subordinate styles.

Gamesman (low deference, high distance, very high divergence)

The Gamesman style is characterized by its extremely low trust for authority and its self-reported very poor relationships with the boss.[1] Gamesmen report, by far, the worst relationship quality of all the styles.

Statistical analysis (see Appendix C) revealed the cluster of items that predicts poor relationships with people in authority. It revealed that the Gamesmen have adopted the perfect formula. They chafe at inequality in the relationship (through a strong sense of their own expertise), are role oriented, and very high on divergence—the factor that, more than any other, seems to determine the quality of the relationship. As a result, they commonly report being in a virtually constant struggle with the organizational hierarchy and the authority structure.

These are mostly well-educated technical people; in the business world, they are often found in research and development. They push hard on authority in general (not just the boss) and have a strong need to influence the boss, but since their disagreements usually involve basic goals, not just conflict over how to reach agreed ends, Gamesmen are often unsuccessful. This may account for their resigned acceptance of inequality and status differences with the boss. They are the very picture of the reserved technical manager who operates in a detached manner, maintaining high personal distance.

Because of the extremely high divergence orientation, which lends an adversarial cast to the relationship with the boss, for Gamesmen political complexity, strategy, and threat define organizational life. They feel that people in authority are not allies, and are even competitors prone to take credit for the subordinates' work. To the Gamesmen, the boss is unlikely to have any concern for their needs, which means they must be self-protective at all times.

Gamesmen seem to look at the organization the way chess players view the pieces on a board. With their generally strong grounding in technical skills and confidence in their own expertise, they do not opt for direct confrontation with the structure and the boss but tend to be more the issues-oriented organizational guerrilla. The boss may be seen as an enemy but, in a sense, is more of an obstruction, an obstacle to be navigated around. Gamesmen do not usually feel a personal antagonism toward the boss or the organization; rather they are expressing a philosophy about hierarchical relationships.

Rebel (low deference, low distance, high divergence)

Rebel subordinates are young, typically very well educated, and low in the organizational hierarchy. They are more often found in educational organizations, social service organizations, and consulting, and are less common in business, government, and health care organizations. When they are found in business, they are most often in engineering, least often in finance and accounting. They report generally poor relationships with people in authority, but not to the degree that the Gamesman does.

Rebels are low-deference subordinates who usually telegraph their approach to their bosses through obviously contentious and argumentative behaviors. Rebels are inclined to define their role as one of challenge, to be a devil's advocate, to keep people in authority honest, even to the point of taunting them. They constantly push and will often use their authority relationships as a foil for purposes of stimulation, dominance struggles, and to gauge their own developing competencies.

Their resistance to deferring is not based on a conviction about their specific expertise but rather is a more personal resistance to structure and a frustration with the constraint it represents. They commonly espouse democratic values and an ideology of social equality transposed onto the workplace organization. Bosses who adopt many signs of their status will arouse the Rebel, because it is easy to insult this subordinate's assumptions about equality. Although in certain kinds of decision processes the Rebel can provide an invaluable service, if the decision runs counter to his preferences, he can easily become obstructionist.

The nondeferential behavior of Rebels is somewhat softened by their more personal preferences in the boss-subordinate relationship. They are inclined to push for influence, but they are also likely to maintain a more personal sort of contact in the relationship with authority. Though they tend to remain hidden themselves, they solicit disclosure from their bosses, perhaps to gain an advantage. This may create a sort of whiplash effect for the boss, as the Rebel alternately becomes personal and interested and then reverts to using the boss as a foil. It is likely, though, that this personal contact helps the Rebel subordinate to maintain some perspective, balance, and connection in her approaches to the conflict with authority.

Much like the prodigal son or daughter, the orientation of low deference combined with high divergence is likely to promote a fair amount of personally guided and unsanctioned activity by this subordinate. Like Independents, Rebels are sometimes seen as loose cannons by people in authority. However, since their disagreements are usually aimed at methods, not goals, and because they tend to be obvious in their disagreement, their activities do not tend to undermine the boss very much.

Overall the Rebels will be viewed differently in different organizational cultures or functional subcultures. Looser, organic systems with innovative cultures will likely regard them with amusement and resignation, or even value them as useful in shaking things up and energizing innovative thinking. More traditional and mechanistic cultures are likely to treat them as a sort of invading virus to be contained and neutralized.

Whistleblower (medium-high deference, high distance, high divergence)

Whistleblowers are intriguing because they seem to be like the Military style but with a sudden shift into high divergence. This suggests the solid organizational citizen who has a very low tolerance level for organizational malfeasance, misdeeds, and omissions. As such, Whistleblowers stand out once their values are stretched beyond the ethical breaking point. They are generally cooperative but eternally wary and vigilant.

Whistleblowers are frequently found in health care, business, and social service organizations. They are rare in military and government organizations. They are frequently found in research and development, show up quite often in production and management information systems, and are infrequently found in human resources, finance, or accounting.

Externally, Whistleblowers look to be solid, unremarkable organizational citizens. Generally, they are agreeable and nonthreatening. However, it would be, and often is, a mistake to over-look the strong ethical streak that functions as their internal gyro-scope. Though most often they ultimately defer to the boss in decision processes and accept the authority structure, Whistleblow-ers have an undercurrent of strong values, conviction about their own expertise, and a relentless fix on organizational and social goals.

They seem to be constantly calculating the alignment between the boss's apparent goals and the organizational goals. In the pres-ence of difference or conflict, the Whistleblower prefers matters to be resolved by reference to objective standards and tenets of pro-fessional conduct. This subordinate will therefore, more than likely, opt for traditional and accepted problem-solving approaches until becoming convinced that this will not work.

Once they realize that their solid, "by the book" approach is get-ting nowhere, Whistleblowers can, overnight, accomplish a star-tling and often precipitous shift into a confrontational and rigid stance. Their high-deference orientation leads them away from a lot of argument with organizational authorities. Instead, due to their high degree of divergence, they will when frustrated resort to out-side forms of resolution to accomplish what they are convinced is right. This is likely to result in a surprising escalation of ideological conflict with very little warning.

Managers with this orientation often see themselves as serving their organizations and society in general. Indeed, as we review many of the famous cases of whistleblowing, the extent to which these subordinate managers tried to solve problems within the cur-rent structure is impressive. Their decisions to go public with their complaints often come as a last resort, when they decide their orga-nizations will do nothing to avert danger to the organization, its stakeholders, and the larger society.

Reactions to Rebels and Whistleblowers

It is useful to pause a moment here and contrast the Rebel and Whistleblower styles in terms of the likely reactions they will elicit from their bosses. Their differing orientations to divergence and distance mean that, when in conflict, the two styles are likely to be seen much differently. Where the Rebel is personal, her behavior can be seen by an indulgent authority as that of the errant (or prodigal) daughter. The Whistleblower's strong role orientation, on the other hand, helps to escalate differences with the boss to ideological (and often insoluble) proportions quickly. His behavior is much less likely to be smiled at, understood, or forgiven.

The nature of disagreement is also different for the two styles. Rebels most often disagree over methods and procedures (*how* we do things), while Whistleblowers more often refer to goal conflicts (*what* things we are doing). The latter difference is more profound.

Rebel attacks on the authority structure of the organization are usually obvious and suggest a righteousness that, while contentious, stops short of rejecting fundamental assumptions of the organization. The Rebel struggles more against the means or methods to achieve largely acceptable goals or outcomes. For Whistleblowers, it is precisely these goals that are in question, and their actions can come to represent a more fundamental attack on the entire system. While problematic for their organizations since (when they actually do blow the whistle) they often lose their jobs and careers, Whistleblowers perform an ultimately invaluable service for their organizations and society.

While overall measures of relationship quality suggest roughly the same quality for each group, these conceal several important points of contrast:

1. It is likely that the Whistleblowers overestimate their relationship quality more so than the Rebels because high relationship distance tends to worsen conflict with their bosses.

2. In the measures of relationship quality with authority, Rebels report greater feelings of success and effectiveness with authority than do the Whistleblowers. However, the Rebels report a poorer ongoing relationship climate. For them, the climate is stormier and more turbulent, since they are often in explicit, or overt, struggle.

3. For the Whistleblower the reverse is true. They report a more positive relationship climate (since on the surface they are generally agreeable) but much less feeling of ultimate effectiveness, given the profound nature of their differences with people in authority.

Now that you have a clearer picture of yourself and how you manage your relationships with people in authority, Chapter Six will tell you what you should do with this new understanding. The basic message is, Hold onto your existing orientation. But, since there are bound to be some drawbacks to it and situations in which it does not serve you well, learn how to complement it with other approaches.

One of the exciting things about these nine styles is that each has its own unique and practical aspects and each is perfectly appropriate in some situations. Learn from each and build new competencies into *your* style. Be versatile and adjust depending on the tasks you and your boss face.

Chapter Six

Being More Effective with Bosses: Adaptations of Style

> The point is, instead of my style being a familiar and comfortable groove, a reflex, it needs to be more like an adjustable tool, something that needs to be adjusted to the work my boss and I do together.
>
> —*An executive in the research project*

Now that you have a basic understanding of the different ways people approach being a subordinate, and some idea of your own style, we can turn to the most important point of this book: even though you probably do have a consistent subordinate style, you can learn to become more flexible in your approach to being a subordinate, and in so doing, you—and your boss—can become more effective.

But wait—can you really change? Some people have doubts that adults can change something as deeply seated as the orientations and approaches we have been discussing. So, before going any further, let us deal with the question of whether or not people can alter their behavior in the ways I have been suggesting.

Can You Really Change?

While some people think that much of an adult's behavior is hard-wired and therefore cannot be changed, I think most of what and who we are is the result of things we have learned. Most of our behavior has been learned over the course of our lives in response to our needs and to the situations we have found ourselves in. Some of this behavior we may have learned recently, but a great deal of it was learned when we were small children and adolescents. This is true of our learning about how to relate to people in authority.

Much of the way we behave toward people in authority was learned as children when we learned to deal with our mothers and fathers—the first authority figures most of us had. As we moved into schools and later into employing organizations, further lessons probably reinforced and, to some extent, changed that learning.

We may not even recall how we came to believe the things that we believe. Because the learning took place long ago, we may no longer be aware of how or when or why we learned what we did. This may account for why we feel that some learning is hard-wired. It seems as if it has always been part of us, somehow encoded in the very fabric of our personality.

Such early learning is certainly powerful, but it is not the end of learning. Nor should it be. In fact, behavior learned long ago is often not well suited to our present life and circumstances.

In all kinds of ways, when we go out into the world, we learn that some of our early learning does not suit us anymore. The lives we lead, the relationships we have, and the situations we choose to be part of often demand that we fashion new ways to behave. In many ways, we learn how to adapt, to alter our behavior—sometimes even our beliefs—to be more in keeping with our adult identity and adult activities. As adults in the adult world, we are called upon to learn new things every day, to adjust our behavior and sometimes our ways of thinking.

Actually, we adjust our behavior quite a bit. There are some situations and settings where, without changing fundamental preferences or leanings, our surface behavior changes all the time. For example, at work, when engaged in problem solving, we are likely to call forth our reasoning skills, objectively analyze a work problem, and strive to approach it relatively unemotionally. Organizations tend to support and reward this sort of behavior. To a work colleague who has just received disappointing news about an expected promotion, we might offer support and words of encouragement, express our confidence in them, maybe offer a little strategic counsel. Then later, when we arrive home, we find out our young son or daughter has broken a favorite toy and is distraught over it. As a parent, we might offer our sympathy and concern, or just hold and try to comfort a crying child.

Some of these behaviors may be more difficult for us to do than others, since we are likely to prefer one way of relating over another. But, to a greater or lesser extent, we learn how to adjust our behavior to the situation.

In the same way, recent leadership theory has instructed managers that no one way of leading is going to be best in all situations. An effective manager must adapt her approach to the situation. This means a manager must recognize that a situation requires different behavior or skills, and then must know how to call forth what is required. To be effective leaders in different situations, managers must learn how to adapt leadership style and be situationally flexible.

To be effective subordinates, managers must learn how to do the same thing with their subordinate style. This does not mean that you must alter your fundamental predisposition, but it does suggest determining what your "reflex" is and then learning how to be more versatile in your behavior. You may always prefer, and be more comfortable in, a certain kind of relationship with your bosses. However, it is important to recognize when (in what situations) that relationship is not well suited to the tasks you face. In those situations, effectiveness requires you to adapt, or change, your behavior.

If I have a leaning toward high deference, for example, I may always believe that respectfully deferring to the boss is an important value. As a subordinate, an important part of my role and my identity is to be a loyal and effective implementer of my boss's directives. I am likely to feel most like myself when I do that. Acting some other way toward the boss may feel forced, false, and not like me.

Yet I can and I must learn to recognize when my reflexive behavior is not the best for the task I am attempting. To do this, I must first learn to recognize when indulging my preference will get in the way of effectiveness.

This requires an ability to recognize situations that may call for a different approach—a situational awareness. For example, if my boss and I are engaged in a creative task, perhaps brainstorming alternatives to a problem, I must notice that my reflexive and accustomed approach is likely to be ineffective. It will not help with the task at hand. Instead of two minds engaged in a dynamic exchange, we will only have one—my boss's—working on our problem.

Then I must learn the behavioral skills that help me do what is better suited to the situation. I must engage in lively give-and-take, push back, perhaps even argue against my boss for my ideas. I must know how to do what will best serve the task; I must engage in the right behavior.

Situational Demands

Of course, we work in organizations that tend to support some ways of thinking and behaving while discouraging others. And, since our relationship with our bosses *is* a relationship, the way the boss thinks and behaves is also important.

In a number of ways, I consider myself a private person. When I am at work with my boss, I focus my energies on the task at hand. However, when my development is at issue, I recognize that this is a situation in which I must act counter to my normal preferences. I need to talk more openly with my boss about my aspirations, anxieties, fears, and hopes.

Yet personal disclosure tends to make my boss uncomfortable. One day I told him that I noticed some uneasiness in him. He admitted that personal conversations did make him a bit uncomfortable. I went on to explain why I thought he needed to know these things and why we needed to discuss them. It was a good talk, and he agreed with me. Both of us, it would appear, are acting a little against our grain, but the outcomes are clearly positive, both for us as a team and for my access to development opportunities.

While acting counter to our preferences may feel awkward at first, after we have developed, or rounded out, our "flat sides," more behaviors will feel comfortable, if not natural. Then, with equal facility, we can move toward either pole of deference, distance, and divergence as the situation demands.

So, in the relationship with your boss, an important part of this kind of change may be some dialogue, perhaps even some negotiation. (Let him read some sections of this book!) Perhaps the next performance evaluation is a good time to give your relationship to the boss some explicit attention and discussion.

At this point you may be thinking you do not need to change much because you always get along well with your boss. Bear in mind that many managers confuse getting along with the boss (we like each other, feel friendly, joke a lot, and so on) with being an effective team. These are different things. Getting along well, while important, should not be your highest aspiration. You can get along well with your boss and still be ineffective as a working pair.

If just getting along with the boss was your only concern, you could maximize your chances of doing that by adopting a style with high deference, middle to low distance, and low divergence—essentially the Military or Partisan style.[1] But even though these styles are common in business and quite useful in the right situations, in many ways they do not address the critical issues facing today's organizations.

Consider, for instance, the demands that shortened product and service life cycles have placed on organizations for increased innovation and creativity. While the Military and Partisan styles suggest good implementation skills, such skills are not likely to lead to many new ideas. Nor as a general rule are managers using these styles comfortable in taking risks. In the newer, flatter, more organic systems, workers at all levels must learn to become initiators and be willing and able to act, when appropriate, without upper management direction.

Another example of the situational demands for more flexible subordinate styles is downsizing. Our organizational future clearly involves reduced numbers and layers in management. Managers at all levels will be unable to oversee and monitor their subordinate managers as they may have done in the past. Subordinate managers will need to be more autonomous and, within guidelines, to take initiative and risk. This need for autonomy and initiative, supported by relentless demands to be globally competitive, cannot be met by boss-subordinate pairs who operate under a traditional "tell and do" approach to their relationship. Bosses need to create conditions for subordinate manager success, and subordinate managers will have to accept new responsibilities.

If our organizations are to survive and to prosper amid these demands, the partners in this key boss-subordinate relationship must look carefully at how well their relationship creates synergy and enhances task accomplishment. Equating success with getting along well, or with being comfortable in the relationship, is not likely to be effective.

A Guide to Developing Flexibility

The best way to develop flexibility in your approach to being a subordinate manager is to learn to recognize those situations that would be better handled with a style different from your usually and accustomed approach.

Not every situation lends itself to a low-deference, push-back-hard kind of approach. Some situations call for more deference for the boss. For example, a high-deference situation is one in which deferring to the boss is likely to make you, the boss, and the two of you as a team, more effective. There are thus high- and low-deference situations, as well as high- and low-distance and high- and low-divergence situations. What are the differences among these various situations? How can you recognize them? That is what this section is all about.

But first let us be very clear on this: I am not suggesting that you should abandon or stop using an existing set of skills. Rather, the goal is to complement, or add to, that existing set of skills with its opposite partner. If you tend toward being consistently high or low on deference, distance, or divergence, learn the practical uses of the complementary approach, and learn how to behave using it.

Recognizing High-Deference Situations

Whether your style preference is for high or low deference, it will be useful to recognize those situations in which higher deference may be more effective. With this recognition, a high-deference manager in the following situations can exercise his natural approach with confidence that it is probably effective. Much more important, however, a manager with an accustomed *low*-deference approach will learn the situations in which pushing for influence may not make as much sense and lead to more ineffective outcomes.

Thus the low-deference manager should pay special attention to the following situations where high deference is called for:

- *In a crisis.* When time is short and action is the first consideration, taking the time to push back and seek influence can slow decision making. If the problem analysis is completed, being an effective implementer may be the best choice.

- *When the stakes are low and the problem definition is clear.* In these situations, pushing for influence may be a waste of energy and time, since there is very little you can use your influence to accomplish that would not happen anyway. Do not use every decision event as a test of your influencing skills.

- *When the outcomes of the decision are not likely to go against or contradict your values.* In these situations you are likely to be able to live with whatever decision the boss may make. There is no need to work for influence, since you have no clear personal stake in the decision either for its direct impact or as precedent.

• *When you have no specialized knowledge or unique perspective.* If you really have little, in comparison, to offer, do not push for influence just to see if you can get it. This is being merely oppositional.

• *When the boss is clearly an expert.* If the problem lends itself to the boss's expertise and yours is not as extensive, let the boss make the decision. Be the naive questioner, learn something, then defer.

• *When there are larger factors or considerations.* In some situations you will not be a good judge because there are factors beyond your knowledge operating, and you do not know how they might bear on the decision. The boss is probably the best judge at such times.

• *When your boss does not react well to being pushed.* This situation requires judgment. Some bosses never react well, but when a boss objects and the relationship cannot take the stress at that time, or when the issue is not worth the stress, deferring to the boss may be more effective. Outside the press of an immediate decision situation, try to discuss this behavior with your boss as one of your responsibilities. Set the stage for future exchanges if at all possible.

• *When your colleagues are in agreement with the boss, and there is little to be gained by further argument.* Sometimes you will need to recognize that you have failed in your attempts at influencing. It is fair to ask the boss to restate, in her own words, what you have argued for, to make certain you were heard, but then give it up. You may ultimately be proved right, but set the stage for influence at a later date. You have lost this one. Be as gracious as you can.

When you do defer, try to stay informed about the outcome and the effects of the decision and the decision quality. Suggest a point at which some evaluation will take place. Try not to drop out of, sabotage, or relinquish responsibility for decision outcomes that go against you. To do this legitimizes others doing the same thing when it is your solution that is adopted.

Talk with your boss. If it turns out that it was a good decision, see what you can learn about how to make and implement such decisions. If it turned out badly, learn together about what happened and file it away for future reference. If deferring to the boss results in a string of bad decisions, you will need to provide stronger low-deference support for your boss.

One final word to the low-deference manager: Do not overreact if the boss likes symbols and the trappings of authority. Though such preferences may be a clue to his inner workings and values, try to stay more carefully attuned to how he behaves in relation to you. Overlook some of the form in favor of the substance of your relationship.

Recognizing Low-Deference Situations

These are the situations in which the naturally high-deference subordinate manager may become relatively ineffective. Learn to recognize those times when pushing for more influence can make you and your boss—and the two of you as a team—more effective in your work together. If you are already a low-deference manager, these are the situations where your style will likely add value to the decision process with your boss.

Remember in reading this that most subordinate managers tend to overestimate (in comparison to how their bosses rate them) how much they push back against their bosses. Managers who see themselves as vigorously arguing a point of view can be surprised to learn that their bosses perceive a rather tentative or even tepid argument. You might want to find out how the boss sees you on this dimension. You may have more room to push back than you think.

When should you move toward lower deference to the boss?

• *When problem definition is not clear.* When you do not know what you are facing, even in crisis situations, it is good to get multiple perspectives on the table. Pushing points of view can be helpful in establishing some clarity about the "best fit" definition. But do not overdo it to the point that more heat than light results.

• *When it is a high-stakes issue and is likely to have a large impact on you.* If there are important outcomes for your organization, your larger community, or you and potentially your career, get in there! You will have to live with its consequences. Act responsibly.

• *When there appears to be a values clash.* Some decision outcomes or contemplated alternatives clash with your basic values. These can be uncomfortable moments, but ethical concerns have an increasingly important place in decision making. Such concerns are more often appropriately handled by you inserting them into the decision-making process. You may enable others to raise similar concerns and save your boss, decision team, organization, and community from disaster.

• *When you have specialized knowledge or a unique perspective that bears on the problem.* When you have a well-informed view, make certain it gets heard. Do your homework. If you feel strongly about it, say so and back it up. You will add value, which, after all, is what you are paid to do.

• *When there is a high demand for creativity.* This describes a lot of decision situations. Creativity depends on your promoting your ideas and being a foil for the ideas of others. Challenge yourself and your boss to think new thoughts. Do not be afraid to argue against a point of view (yours, a colleague's or your boss's) or to tell your boss why you think her idea is a great one, even—especially—when she herself may not think much of it.

• *When you foresee significant difficulty in implementing the decision.* Do not simply salute and march out confused or daunted. Voice implementation concerns and insist they be addressed. An elegant but undoable solution is a bad solution. The boss may have ready answers. Do not be cagey about it: clearly say what problems you expect to encounter and get help. That is the boss's job too.

• *When you have taken on the devil's advocate role, either at your own or your boss's suggestion.* Do not always be the one to play it, but you can contract to be the personal conscience of your boss and your decision team. In your advocacy role, push your boss and others to defend their proposals. It is a good service. Do it well, with conviction and balance.

• *When you cannot see (even indirectly) other larger factors that are driving the decision.* This can be a tough call. I said before that if larger considerations were in play that your boss had to consider, deferring to the boss might be the best option. However, if you fear that argument is being used as a smokescreen, try to find out if such factors genuinely exist, and then make a decision. If your boss has had a good track record with you and has been forthcoming and honest, then defer. If the clear record, not just your dark suspicions, has been filled with information suppression, half truths, or outright lies, then do not defer. If you are overruled, you might want to record your exception in a memo to the boss (and the file).

• *When there are developmental reasons.* All subordinate managers need to develop a comfort with, and a commitment to, their own ideas and learn how to move them by getting them into the decision mix. After all, it is part of the requirement and the training for higher-level work, and it can expose you to critical thought processes and aid in learning more refined and effective influencing skills. As one executive remarked:

> Operating with high deference to authority is a staple for me that I have been slowly moving away from. (I believe two years ago I would have been way up the scale.). . . It will allow me to become more comfortable in carrying out my own intuitive strategies and to be a more independent thinker. I can see the improvement opportunities in being less deferential to authority.

Some general advice about operating from a low-deference orientation will help you and your boss be more effective in this mode.

First, if you feel you must challenge and push your boss, try to put in something new. A low-deference executive had this to say:

> The potential difficulty that I have to watch is appearing to negate ideas when they're put forth by superiors. The "devil's advocate" role in decision making can be positive, but honest comments both in the negative and the affirmative must be made while assuring others that I'm trying to help the organization and individuals improve.

Do not oppose, or be seen as opposing, for the mere sake of opposition, thereby turning the decision situation into a test of wills or a test of power. Be careful to voice support and agreement as readily and as energetically as you voice your independent views. When you like and support a decision, say so clearly and explain why. This will model good behavior for others. It will also create a sort of relationship cushion for you and your boss when you feel compelled to push in other directions, to disagree. It is likely to get you more influence since it will become difficult to stereotype (and dismiss) you as negative, a naysayer, not a team player.

Second, be careful to confine your challenges to work-related, issue-related matters. Try not to let it get personal. Address the consequences of proposed actions for the task. Reason from your expertise, knowledge, understanding of the situation, and the data you base your views on. Try to find out (if you do not know) what knowledge or priorities your boss is operating with. If it is a values conflict, try to resolve it by reference to the goals and values of the organization.

And be careful not to develop an investment in proving your boss wrong or "one-upping" the boss. Even if you win this time, remember it is likely to be a long season with lots of other situations to be faced. For the long term, you need to create more of a partnership.

Third, sense and remember the limits of the culture of your organization for tolerating this sort of activity. This is not to say you should throttle yourself if you have a well-founded position; just do not be naive about the type and amount of support you will get at other levels. As one executive wrote:

> If I am going to be effective in work situations with my superiors, I must understand that it is one thing to defer to them for the sake of getting on with the job and not fighting a losing battle after I make my case. On the other hand, it is quite another thing to defer to superiors simply as a way of avoiding conflict with them; something that . . . I have the capacity to do. Furthermore, the idea or insight that I hold back from superiors to avoid a conflict with them may just be the one that makes a situation possible, and will not be perceived as a challenge at all.

Recognizing High-Distance Situations

There are situations that call for a different approach to managing personal distance in the relationship with your boss. The following section will highlight situations where orienting yourself to a high-distance approach makes sense and will be more effective.

If you are already inclined to this approach, you may see the elements of your logic here. This is where your approach should work pretty well. The manager whose approach is to low distance should pay particular attention here, since I will point out when you should shift into a different approach. Learn to recognize these situations and adapt your behavior.

When should you move toward higher distance with your boss?

• *When personal disclosure creates undesirable vulnerability.* Higher distance makes sense if you and your boss work in a *highly* politicized work environment where decisions are based less on data and more on who wants what and who has the power. Under this circumstance, self-disclosure can be naive, impractical, or even dangerous. The information can be used against you.

• *When confidences are not respected, and you have clear data that supports this.* Be careful and be selective but find people in whom you can confide. Work can become very stressful and lonely if you maintain high distance everywhere. Find someone to talk to. If one of these people is not your boss, you are in big trouble. Confront it if at all possible. Finding alternative higher-level sponsors, while sometimes risky, may be a good option.

• *When your boss has a high-distance orientation and the culture of your function or organization supports it.* This is not to say you must cater to this, but your boss's resistance to lessening distance must be considered. If this is the case, you might want to lessen the amount or richness of information you turn over, consider the setting (go out to lunch instead of talking in the office), or use a "cooler" medium such as written memos. You can also try to have a conversation about why, for task reasons, the boss should at least know a few things about your excitements, your aspirations, relevant family and other aspects of your life external to work. This is a case in which you may need to be the instructor.

• *When time is pressing.* This assumes that task issues (not development or appraisal or job assignments) are uppermost. Getting the job done is the most pressing issue. Keep your personal self out of it. The task focus is likely to prevent your boss from joining with you anyway.

- *When a problem is transitory.* If you believe a personal problem or issue affecting you is going to be passing quickly and there will likely be no noticeable or enduring impact on you at work, do not introduce it into your relationship with your boss. Use your friends and family for support.

Remember too that regardless of the distance you maintain, either by reflex or by choice, there is no need to be cold or graceless to others, especially your boss. Do not overpolarize your choices here. You can take an interest in the boss if she desires it or seems to respond well to inquiries. Be friendly. Even though you may choose to withhold detailed personal information, you can let the boss know when you are suffering the effects of a personal problem, have had a great success, or are just feeling down.

If you are in the grip of some personal difficulty, you might warn the boss that she might notice some unusual behavior or drop in your output. Where work effects are inevitable, your boss has a right to *some* information. And you would be foolish not to offer it. Managers often overestimate how well they are concealing and coping with personal problems. You may be able to get the space or the help you need without deep disclosure.

Recognizing Low-Distance Situations

The following are situations where lower distance has importance and relevance. If your orientation is already to maintain low distance, this is how and when your orientation works for you. If you are oriented to maintain high distance in the relationship with your bosses, take note. These are the situations where you will need to complement, or round out, your style.

Remember that personal disclosure is not absolute; it is not a question of either being completely closed up or totally open. Those are the extremes; you have many choices in between. Consider bounded and managed openness. In certain contexts or situations, engage in appropriate and role- or task-related disclosure. It is your right not to place in full view of your boss (and others) non-work-related aspects of your personal life. For those you like and trust, you may choose to do so for purely personal reasons. This is a matter of personal preference.

However, note that certain kinds of personal information have a direct bearing on your development as a manager and your abilities to carry out work, particularly in team-oriented cultures. Newer management approaches are promoting and supporting less personal distance with less formal relationships. Upper-level managers are asking other levels of management to develop more appreciation of top management's core values and interests and how those values are to be implemented through other managers' largely autonomous action. In effect, they are saying, "Develop a sense of how I go about making decisions, what I value, what I am hoping to accomplish."

I am reminded of the Disney Corporation, where, when struggling with a problem, managers often can be heard to ask, "What would Walt do?" or "What would Walt want?" In this way managers are attempting to take a more intuitive orientation to their founder's values and world view. It is a more personal appreciation.

You should reduce personal distance in the following circumstances:

• *When your development is at issue.* If the boss is going to share in responsibility for your development, he should know some things about who you are, what interests you have, what excites and motivates you, what your dreams and aspirations are, what causes you to feel anxious, how you cope with being overwhelmed, where you see yourself going, what are your values, and how you like to learn. The boss will also be helped by having some understanding of your life structure and the responsibilities that *you* see as having a bearing on your availability for certain kinds of work or for certain assignments.

Some of this information might be inferred in the course of normal work. Some of it might come out in other types of exchanges. But however it comes to the surface, the main point is, the boss needs it, you need to talk about it, and the boss needs to take it in.

Even an executive who scored quite high in distance offered this acknowledgment:

> I have decided that while I value my privacy, particularly in the work setting, I want my boss to like me, to take a personal interest in me and my development. . . . I also am . . . a caring individual . . . for those above me as well as subordinates and peers.

• *When formal, or informal appraisals occur.* Whether in the formal periodic appraisal, or in daily and weekly appraisal, if there are things impinging on work performance, you need to keep the boss aware. If a divorce is in progress, a child is being born, a graduation pending, a parent is near death, or there are some health problems, alert your manager so that it can be considered in reviewing your activities. This can also help adjust expectations, plan for substitutions, or provide help for you if you should require time off or be incapacitated. Under such circumstances your work habits are likely to be altered, so the boss is likely to notice something is going on anyway.

• *When you want into the backstage information loop.* Kitchen talk, interactions at the golf course, or gatherings at the corner diner for coffee in the morning, while ostensibly social, usually include a lot of backstage information and negotiation of work arrangements. Sharing some out-of-work personal interests can set the stage for these useful, career-enhancing outings. One executive noted:

> Important information, in today's business world, is often exchanged through personal exchanges—for example, on the golf course. Distance can take personal factors out of a decision process, but emotion and value integrated decisions can be more effective.

• *When you are pushing your boss hard for influence.* Aggressive nondeference produces fewer problems or side effects when there is less distance between you and your boss. A personal connection dramatically lessens or softens the alienating aspects of your being strongly inner directed.

• *When you are seeking greater relationship security and reduction of stress.* Low distance can provide greater feelings of security and form a relationship cushion to handle criticism or conflict (whether it is developmental or "disciplinary" in nature) and stress. An executive commented:

> Just being able to talk with [my boss] really helped me to deal with a personal crisis. He understood better why I seemed to be a bit off at times, and when he needed to bring some of my "less than excellent" work to my attention, he did it with sensitivity. I felt the support and the space . . . and it made it easier to take the criticism . . . and to do something about the problems that were raised.

• *When task assignments are being considered.* You must decide what aspects of your life you want to be considered here. Perhaps if your daughter or son is about to graduate or your spouse is ill, you are clear that you want to be near home. This is not the best time for your boss to send you off on that two-week trip to a supplier or client far away, so let the boss know of your preferences. If you go, you are likely to be less effective. If the boss is not aware of your situation, she may inadvertently worsen your problems. Perhaps the trip can be rescheduled or someone else can go. Or, if it has to be you, perhaps you can get some backup or greater staff support or get extra travel allowances for a mid-assignment return.

• *When you and your boss are dealing with unstructured problems.* Generally when problems are not resolvable by use of a formula, or a known and established method, decision makers' values enter into the process in a much more significant way than in structured problems. The people behind the roles tend to assert themselves more strongly. When the task of the moment is that kind of problem, or when the tasks of a boss-subordinate pair commonly or frequently include such problems, having a clearer sense of who the parties are, their preferences, biases, enthusiasms, and fears, will make the pair more effective at coming to viable solutions.

• *When emotional facts are important.* A boss's lack of enthusiasm (or yours) for a new product strategy or some other decision can prevent successful implementation of a solution or result in politicizing decisions. Being aware of what the boss's stand is, or how he feels, can help map out directions. Learn the cues to various emotional states. It can often be helpful to identify them, as they may be affecting the decision-making process.

• *When you want richer, more fulfilling contact with people you like and admire.* For many, pursuing greater social contact and satisfaction in the workplace is its own reward.

• *After you and boss have been through some struggles, resulting in strained communications and remoteness.* Try to reestablish contact on a personal level with your boss. Set aside for the moment whatever differences intruded into your interactions and "rehumanize" your boss. To become remote (beyond some cooling off) is likely to make things worse as your imagination takes over. Betty, a controller, discussed a conflict she had with her boss and how it had resulted in a remoteness she found uncomfortable and was getting in the way of their work:

> I will make an effort to reconnect. I think that I would like to do this over lunch, or over drinks after work, but definitely outside the office. The personal side of our relationship needs to be, at least for me, reestablished. This will be difficult for me, since it is also leaving me wide open for rejection. I have to trust my instincts, which tell me that he has as much invested in my active participation in the organization as I do.

Recognizing High-Divergence Situations

In today's organizations, we are finding it increasingly important to emphasize cooperative, collaborative relationships and teamwork. Aligning individual goals and activities with those of the group, and getting both of those in alignment with larger organizational goals, are primary tasks of managers at all levels. Integration of these things makes a low-divergence orientation quite useful and valuable.

However, the requirements for ethical behavior and for organizations to operate with a social consciousness are also on the increase. Sometimes the pressures and interests of those at higher levels lead to unacceptable and even bad decisions when reviewed in a larger values context. While organizations are often quite good at getting everyone working synergistically, certain demands on organizations result in disintegration or even require divergent thinking. Creativity and innovation are two core processes (in addition to ethical behavior) that require a capacity for divergence.

In addition to being cooperative systems, to a greater or lesser extent organizations are also political systems. Managers, while generally promoting alignment or convergence, need to be alert to situations that require or suggest more of a high-divergence orientation. In the following section, those with an orientation to high divergence will see the rationale for the utility of their approach. For those with a low-divergence orientation, here are situations where it is advisable for you to shift to the other side of the scale.

Move toward high divergence in the following situations:

• *When subunit or department goals, activities, and values do not appear to be congruent with larger organizational goals and values*, or, even if they are congruent, when those goals and activities violate your values. Organizational goals, since they are most often public, are generally quite desirable end states to pursue. But since they are public, they often have only a hazy relationship to what is actually going on inside the organization. If your activities, your boss's, and your function's activities seem to have little relationship to those, raise the issue. In the alternative, protect yourself. Let us face it, not all bosses are ethical or honorable. And there are many more who are *mostly* ethical and honorable, but also vulnerable to organizational pressures and periodic lapses into predominantly self-interested behavior.

• *When you are personally responsible for the consequences of your actions,* or even if that potential exists and you are likely to be politically, legally, or morally vulnerable. Increasingly, organizations and managers individually are being called upon to accept personal responsibilities for their actions. Concealing yourself behind "I was just doing what I was told" is ceasing to be much of a defense. Try to imagine before you act what implications your actions will have. If called upon to defend them, what will you say? One executive commented that he imagines himself explaining what he did to his young daughter. If, in his hypothetical exchange, he feels shame, discomfort, or an inability to be convincing to her, he reconsiders taking the action.

• *When there is a high subunit or peer consensus over wrongheadedness of actions.* Keeping your head when all around you may be losing theirs might be a virtue. But ignoring the alarms of your peers is not wise either. Ultimately, it may be your head that is on the block. Presumably, they are as intelligent and as competent as you, and have roughly the same access to information that you do. If they are in general agreement that some course of action is unwise, chances are they are right. And sometimes their concerns might not be evident. Keep in mind that others may be waiting to see if someone will object before they voice their concerns. Research on groups has demonstrated that the tendency of group members to voice divergent views rises dramatically once any member expresses misgivings.

• *When there is no consensus and someone in authority is pushing a questionable option.* Most problems for managers do not come prepackaged. The existence of a problem, its definition, acceptable solution alternatives, and their consequences—these are all arenas where individual perception and self-interest can come into play. When responsibility is being assigned, watch out for your organization, your function, *and* yourself.

• *When you see people in authority taking undue credit for the work of others and, in questionable ways, letting blame fall on the more vulnerable.* There seems to be more of this happening in times of downsizing and retrenchment when everyone becomes fearful about job security. (One observer of the Iran-Contra fiasco summed the situation up neatly: "Only the people who carried out the policy are being indicted. The soldiers will be hung, and the generals will walk"; "Munitions Expert," 1988, p. 5).

• *When your boss appears to be vulnerable, out of favor, or in career trouble.* If this is the case, you are also losing access to information, resources, and sponsorship. If you have had a good relationship with your boss, discuss the situation and what to do. If not, scout around for another source of support—or a new job.

In an overall sense, it is important, particularly in times of change, to stay alert to the alignment between your activities and those of your boss, your function, and the organization. In an earlier chapter, I mentioned that the Whistleblower was constantly calculating the degree of alignment between these things. This is a generally good practice. I encourage all managers to develop and maintain a "strategic literacy" about their organization. As one executive commented:

> I have no trouble accepting a superior's goals when they seem to be in the company's best interest. But the minute those in authority start pursuing their own personal goals at the expense of the company, I find myself becoming a diverger.

In such circumstances, it is usually a good idea to investigate the consequences and ramifications of your actions if you comply. If you are to be like the bombardier, someone who is distant from the consequences of actions he initiates, visit the "bomb site." If other people are to be affected by your actions, listen to the language that is used to refer to them, particularly derogatory language or joking about what is likely to be a negative experience for them. Be sensitive to their dehumanization and take it as a warning sign. It is a key early warning indicator of serious errors about to be made.

Do not assume that authority or authorization will protect you. Consult others where possible, inside and outside the organization. Get legal and moral advice. If you are religious, visit your clergy or some adviser connected to your faith. Discuss the problem (confidentially) with others who know you and are outside your decision context. Get external reference points. A look of horror or consternation on an outsider's face can put a different spin on what seemed perfectly acceptable, if not desirable, from the view inside your organization or decision team.

And carefully examine your own motives if you are, or others suggest you are, a habitually mistrustful subordinate. It can appear that you are someone who fashions participation with the boss around being merely oppositional. I have seen many such subordinates who appear to be acting out some ancient script (historical conflicts with authority) and not paying much attention to the present boss or situation. If you suspect you might be chronically mistrustful, try to figure out what specifically you would need to see in your boss, what behavior, what she would have to do or say to begin earning your trust. If you cannot come up with specific behavioral indicators, suspect a bias on your part.

In most instances and for most purposes, managers can and should operate with reasonable (though not habitual) trust for their bosses. Remember, bosses are likely to react much like anyone else to being constantly mistrusted, subverted, or challenged. If such behaviors seem out of proportion, they are likely to find ways to exclude you from important information and decision making. And, of course, this will likely fuel your mistrust. As a hedge against those times when you feel compelled to diverge, be careful to express joining, to voice agreement and support when you feel those things too.

Avoid the mistake of being silent when you agree and speaking up only when you disagree. From others' perspective, it will lead to a view of you as always being oppositional.

Recognizing Low-Divergence Situations

Most researchers agree that good authority relationships are based on trust. Someone of a highly divergent orientation is less likely to develop trust in the boss.

Consistent divergence will strain a relationship and cause you to lose out on access to resources, information, and choice assignments. Even in a political context, there are bosses who can and should be trusted. And even where you might have seen questionable behavior, perhaps it is confined to certain decision situations; in other situations, you can safely trust your boss. Be careful of your tendency to globalize mistrust (or trust) for your bosses.

If you are oriented to low divergence, the following may be reasons to hold onto that capacity. If you have a high-divergence orientation, here are some situations where you ought to relax your vigilance.

- *When you have investigated consequences and are satisfied that the course of action is acceptable.* Try looking down the road to implementation of decisions and beyond. Are you comfortable with what you see?

- *When your boss has earned your trust* and, as far as you know, is under no new pressures and is not in any career bind. Pay attention to your boss's behavior, choices, and values even on decisions you are not involved in, even on minor issues. They can tell volumes about someone's integrity.

- *When subunit actions are clearly in accordance with larger organizational goals and methods are acceptable to you.* You can see how decisions taken serve legitimate ends.

- *When there is high congruence with your values.* Even when you are not certain about the ends that the decision serves, if the actions themselves conform to your values, this is likely to be an occasion for trust.

- *When the decision makers fully consider outcomes.* If the decision process takes into account impact on the organization and on those who are going to be affected, if the decision team makes an effort to fully understand and make vivid the direct and indirect effects of the proposed actions, this is probably a decision you can get behind.

- *When decision processes and outcomes are subjected to outside review.* Trends toward more informed and activist boards of directors are a good step in this direction. But any form of external review is reassuring. Consultation with labor representatives, or outside groups, as in the example of affirmative action and equal opportunity, provides reassurance of integrity and fairness. Such attention on the decision-making side can also make decisions much easier to implement. If this is in the mix, relax.

- *When there is clear and explicit consensus among peers.* When your alarms are going off, consult with or take in the comments and views of your peer groups. Try voicing your concerns to a trusted peer and see why he is not as concerned as you. But be careful here; the majority is not always right. Groups are subject to their own kinds of wrongheadedness, a fact often ignored by those who promote unqualified use of groups as decision tools. A biographer of Thomas Jefferson noted, "Though he had stressed his reliance on the wisdom of the Congress and the importance of majority rule in the Republic, Jefferson was not prepared to concede that others would always be right when they differed with him, simply because they outnumbered him and his cabinet" (Mapp, 1987, p. 400).

If you are having problems with your boss or others in authority, check goal congruence and compatibility first. Are you on the same track, or at least one that is close and that you and they can accept? Divergence is a powerful explainer. Do not be provoked into being reactive. Help your boss be competent by not subscribing to the silly expectation that bosses will always be aware of what results their actions and directives will bring about. Have the courage to question. Do not let your agreeable nature or your rebelliousness provoke you into unthinking action—or, for that matter, resistance to action.

All subordinate managers should, with respect to divergence, develop an ongoing situational awareness. Organizational trends are requiring all managers, regardless of their functional affiliations, to be literate in all key areas. This involves, as I have said, a strategic literacy, an awareness of your organization in its larger competitive and environmental context. But it also involves literacy in the fiscal, operational, and human resources area as well.

Be alert to the larger situation of your organization at all times and be sensitive to actions and activities that support or detract from its goal attainment, both in the short and long term. Do not always be looking for wrongdoing and investing huge amounts of energy in self-protection.

But do not be naive either. The higher you go in hierarchical systems, the less decisions and activities are controlled by given rules and procedures. In these levels, outcomes are often a result of opinion coalitions that form and reform around new issues and often indistinct problems, preferences, and views of organizational competencies. There may be situations where assumptions about low divergence cause you to be slow to defend your interests or the interests that have been entrusted to you.

Putting It Together: Action Steps

Now that you have some idea of how you could be more flexible in your subordinate approach, how do you go about making behavioral changes? Now that you have some idea of those situations in which you could behave differently, how do you actually begin to change?

Start with some dialogue with your current boss. Find out what your boss thinks of your effectiveness as a pair. Remember that it is one thing to ask, "Do we get along well?" That's important, but not essential. The real question here is, "Are we effective together?" If the boss's answer is yes, find out how he or she judges this effectiveness.

Find out how your boss sees you on each of the three factors. Does your boss's view differ from your view of yourself? (It is likely to be different on the deference orientation.)[2] If so, find out why. If not, then ask, "How well does this approach suit our work together? Should we be acting in different ways in some of our work together?"

Once you develop a plan to bring underused traits into play, establish behavioral indicators that are clear and unambiguous signs that you are doing what you set out to do or that you are *not* doing what you set out to do. If you lean toward being accommodating to the boss, you might decide to work at being more inner directed, pushing for influence. How will you know if you are doing that? And how will you know whether you are doing it well? That is what these indicators can be used for.

Do not leave the monitoring to yourself. Your impressions of yourself are valuable but are likely to be off the mark in terms of how you are perceived by others, particularly your boss. We know only what we intend to convey; as most of us can attest, what is perceived by others is often quite different.

Ideally, make progress a subject of ongoing dialogue with your boss. Get in the habit of sixty-second feedback huddles with your boss after meetings. Contract with and get feedback from your trusted peers on how you are doing in your interactions with your boss.

Continually monitor, get feedback, adjust, evaluate, and monitor again until new, variable patterns become reflexive and shifting your orientation becomes second nature—or at least more comfortable.

Chapter Seven

Reversing the Lens:
Dealing with Different Styles
When You Are the Boss

I can see big differences among my direct reports in
how they relate to me as their boss.
                                    —*An executive in the research report*

Up to this point, we have focused on your role as a subordinate. But
you are also probably a boss yourself, with subordinates of your own.
As you have been reading, you may have been thinking from time
to time about the issue of style in your relationships with your subordinates. In this chapter, I want to turn the focus around and discuss the implications of what you have learned about subordinate
style for the way you manage the people who report to you.

Managing your subordinate managers with sensitivity to their
style, your style, and the tasks you face can help enhance organizational effectiveness and efficiency. On the other hand, ignoring
these relationships, or reflexively adopting a comfortable style, can
have many negative results, including poor decisions, the loss of tal-
ent, and derailing your own career.

Deference and Conflict at Ford

An example of the negative effects of a poorly managed boss-subordinate relationship—and also a rare and powerful glimpse of life
at the top of an organization—is found in David Halberstam's book
The Reckoning (1986), which describes the battle between Henry
Ford II on one side and Lee Iacocca and Hal Sperlich on the other

over the decision to downsize Ford cars in 1976. Ford, of course, was chairman of the Ford Motor Company, Iacocca was the head of Ford-U.S., and Sperlich was Iacocca's deputy for product design. Iacocca and Sperlich had what was sometimes described as a father-son relationship, and they were of one mind in advocating smaller, more fuel efficient cars to compete with foreign imports. He and Iacocca were sure they knew where the company needed to go; Henry Ford, unfortunately, disagreed.

Sperlich was notorious for his exuberant defiance of authority when he found himself in conflict with it. When Iacocca swallowed hard and deferred to the chairman, Sperlich refused to do the same. The battle between Sperlich and Henry Ford not only consumed and wasted their energies and talents for months but polarized the entire organization.

The conflict became a distraction for everyone, including Iacocca; it stopped progress on other fronts and so polarized thinking in the problem-solving process that no middle-range solutions were considered, much less proposed. The outcome was something that Sperlich neither wanted nor expected. Nor was it an outcome that benefited the Ford Motor Company.

Henry Ford announced there would be no Honda engines in Ford cars and no small cars. "Small cars meant small profits," he declared. Ford was interested in profit margins. Sperlich countered that the Packard company had the highest profit margin per car in the industry the year it went out of business. Furthermore, Ford did not like the idea of Japanese engines in American cars. Sperlich was convinced the market was changing and smaller cars were what the American public wanted. Ford was adamant, and Sperlich completely failed in his efforts to influence him. Iacocca warned Sperlich to back off. Time would prove Iacocca and Sperlich right, but Ford, a manager not known for his openness to influence, refused to budge. As Sperlich grew more insistent, Ford became angrier and angrier. The hopelessness of the struggle, in its last few months, seemed to intensify Sperlich's aggressiveness toward all who disagreed. He was relentless, combative, insistent. He let nothing pass unchallenged. Watching him, one friend thought, was like watching someone commit corporate suicide. He bowed to no one, not even Henry Ford II.

For his part, Ford had shown little affection for Sperlich, who seemed less polished than the new, smoother M.B.A.'s that Ford had hired. Sperlich lacked their panache. Now, as Sperlich argued with him regularly, almost as an equal, Ford's distaste grew. At one point Iacocca took Sperlich aside. "Hal," he counseled, "I know you don't think you're telling the chairman that he's full of shit, but it sounds to him—because of your tone and what he's accustomed to—like you're telling him he's full of shit" (Halberstam, 1986, p. 544).

Later, when Ford ordered Sperlich fired, Sperlich was stunned and astonished. He insisted that he had never done anything he was not supposed to do. Henry Ford II and the entire company would receive their punishment later from the American car buyer.

Like many managers, Ford made the error of not listening. He made this mistake, at least in part, because he did not like to be challenged. Ford's need to be deferred to got in the way of a good decision. Because innovation and change were the task, the challenge and push from Sperlich made sense. While more skill in pushing might have helped Sperlich's case, the time had come for Ford to open his own thinking. A boss manager with high control needs bumped against a subordinate manager with a very low-deference (and probably high-divergence) orientation. Their clash in style obscured the demands of the task. Everyone lost.

Working with Managers of Various Styles

In the next section, I will discuss effective approaches to the different styles discussed in earlier chapters. I will pay particular attention to the implications for how you manage and how you encourage your subordinate managers to relate to you.

I will also consider a number of the current trends in organizing, such as demands for innovation, downsizing and retrenchment, and cross-functional cooperation. If you have been involved, for example, in efforts to achieve empowerment, how should you approach subordinate managers who appear to be in the accommodating group? Operating within their preferred style, subordinates in this group prefer structure and direction. How do you change toward more empowerment when your organization has probably been rewarding the accommodating approach?

Or, if you have subordinate managers who appear to be in the autonomous group and your organization is trying to develop more horizontal (cross-functional, in particular) and vertical cooperation and synergy, how can you get and keep these managers linked to others and to more inclusive agendas, creating synergies, when their style preference is to work independently?

Remember that all style approaches have value and are useful in one way or another. The boss manager's challenge is to help subordinate managers hold onto the strengths of a style while avoiding its weaknesses. The ideal is for a subordinate manager to learn how to deploy, at least some of the time, elements of the other styles. The task for you as a boss is to help your subordinates (managers or otherwise) complement or add to their styles, not correct them.

Military, Helper, Diplomat, Partisan: Working with the Accommodative Styles

Subordinates in the accommodative styles are generally cooperative and good at implementation, but are not likely to push their expertise or operate independently of you, the boss. They tend to avoid taking opposing points of view or promoting controversy. Further, they tend to withhold themselves personally, which can deprive the boss of information that might be useful in their development or in enhancing their motivational climate. Keep in mind that most organizations and bosses have conditioned and rewarded subordinate managers for being accommodative, even though it has often not been in their interests to do so.

In general subordinates with the accommodative styles will need some prodding if they are to develop and introduce their own ideas, particularly if this might lead to disagreement with you. You will probably need to go beyond just encouraging these subordinates; you will also need to acknowledge the ideas they do bring forward. Make sure they know you appreciate their thoughts. Tell them when and how their ideas have spurred you to some insight into a problem or contemplated solution. It is important that such feedback be explicit and somewhat detailed, not general.

On the other hand, if you choose not to follow or incorporate their thoughts, ideas, suggestions, or advice, be sure to get back to them and explain why. If you do not, the next time you want their input, it will be that much harder to get. They will be likely to see your encouragement as nothing more than a calculated technique, a kind of managerial political correctness. This could cause them to devalue their own ideas that much more.

You need to strike a balance with the accommodative styles: Value their "solid citizen" character and loyalty but get them to wake up a little. Push them to be more disciplined in their thinking and analysis, especially the Helper. This will help provide a better foundation for self-assertion. Put them into situations where they are required to think more for themselves. Perhaps have them lead a project team with only light monitoring. They will need to feel you as the boss behind them, interested and supportive, but not crowding or micromanaging. Development might also include deliberate exposure to new trends and ideas and a role in keeping others in the organization up to date on these changes.

For the most part expect subordinates in the accommodative styles to be reluctant to disclose their inner thoughts. They are inclined (except for the Helper) to keep to themselves or be cautious. You might be able to bring them out through occasional relaxed conversations. Offer some of your own thoughts about things that interest or puzzle you. Ask for their ideas, even prod a little, but do not push. Remember to keep a balance. Do not set about changing them or their preferred mode of operating. Instead, recognize their preference for structure and direction and then gradually help them round out their flat sides. Help them complement, or add to, their skill set.

One exception to this general advice on the accommodative styles needs to be offered in the case of the Partisan. Remember that these subordinates are especially eager to please the boss, and their enthusiasm may cause them to go overboard. As Sperlich was to Iacocca in the Ford example, they may be more attached to you, their boss, than to the organization and end up doing things that are in neither's long-term interest.

Be perfectly clear about the tasks you are assigning to Partisan subordinates. Make sure they understand the limits to their discretion by having them confirm their instructions. In addition, try to convey more than the tasks you want completed. Work to get across your intentions and the values you want to maintain throughout the process of working together. Agree on check-in points and make sure you know what they are doing through discreet inquiries. Again, this is a balancing act. You do not want to squash their gung-ho enthusiasm but you do want to help them get their internal gyroscope functioning so that they can develop a better balance between exercising judgment and being advocates.

Independent, Counselor: Working with the Autonomous Styles

Subordinates in the autonomous styles are good at self-guided activity with minimal supervision. People with these styles are generally happiest when working independently on defined tasks that allow them, once they have their instructions, to operate with relative freedom and almost total discretion. The downside of this ability to operate independently is that they are often not well aligned with (or even aware of) larger goals. Furthermore, subordinates in the autonomous styles often resist even appropriate monitoring by authority.

They can be a great assist in cross-functional activities, since many seem to be natural boundary spanners who resist seeing their organizational world exclusively through the lens of their home function.

Subordinates with these styles need to get recognized for their work. They often feel their efforts are overlooked and underappreciated. They tend to mistrust upper-management support, which means they might mistrust your support.

In general, autonomous subordinates will need to learn how to cooperate in a context larger than their own interests. Although they are usually excellent individual contributors and are often good team leaders, they can lose sight of larger agendas and priorities and the need for cooperative synergies. Working in cooperative structures (and constraints) is not something that comes naturally to them, as it does to more accommodative subordinates.

Their most consistent feature is their low-deference orientation. These subordinates need to have influence with you, and it would be wise to allow them this influence. In return, you can insist that they meet three criteria:

1. They must be supremely knowledgeable in their task domain. You will, of course, need to provide the resources for them to develop this level of expertise.

2. They must maintain an alertness and sensitivity to larger goals and priorities. Make certain they hear and take in news about shifting priorities and goals. Discuss how their work might be affected.

3. They must agree to periodic reports and check-ins. These are necessary so that you can channel necessary resources and

information to them and so that you will not be surprised from elsewhere by news of their activities. In those check-ins, become an excellent questioner. Pose questions such as "How do you plan to handle . . . ?" "Did you know about . . . ?" "What do you need from me?" and "I am concerned about X. Are you?"

Be careful not to let any conflicts get heated, since these subordinates are likely to go to great lengths to get their way. To repeat, be especially certain that autonomous subordinates receive all due credit for their work and their contributions. If you are not effective politically, this can be a very difficult relationship to manage.

As we have already seen, women tend to fall more often into the autonomous styles and usually score low on deference. They are more inner-directed than their male counterparts and often mistrusting and self-protective because of a shared common experience of harassment and discrimination. They tend to be wary of developmental contact for fear of exploitation and their trust being abused.

Managers of women managers should take care in asking for their input. When their advice is not taken, make especially certain to get back to them with fuller explanations. This can enhance trust and promote development of the subordinate managers' thinking. Be careful also to establish the *developmental* intimacy that is necessary for mentoring, sponsoring, and development. Do not avoid appropriate personal dialogue, but draw a clear line for yourself that at all times precludes your actions from being interpreted as romantic or overly familiar.

Gamesman, Rebel, Whistleblower: *Working with the Adversarial Styles*

Subordinates in the adversarial styles are generally good at brainstorming, creativity, and innovation. They also serve quite easily in the devil's advocate role and can act as a sort of moral compass for the organization. They are effective organizational "outriders." Since they can easily separate themselves from you and their colleagues, they can easily become isolated and suffer large losses in influence and connection. With an unalert boss, their more contentious styles can also lead to escalated, distracting, and ultimately unproductive conflicts.

Working with subordinates in this group of styles is not as difficult as the adversarial label implies. Do not assume that your best approach is to counter their adversarial tendencies and civilize these subordinates. Also, do not make the opposite mistake of putting them in the devil's advocate role all the time. Instead, your task is to balance their strengths by making sure that they maintain the threads of connection to the organizational mainstream.

Organizations would probably be well served by having more of these types at higher levels, particularly in forming plans and strategies as well as innovation. As the boss, you will need to help sponsor their projects and channel their energies.

Like the Partisan in the accommodative group, the Gamesman is a special case in the adversarial group. Discreetly cultivate your own peer sources to keep abreast of the maneuvering of these subordinate managers. You might even casually let slip that you are aware of their activities.

Gamesmen are generally committed to a view of the organization-as-jungle. Convince them that the two of you can create an island of safety to be more effective. Failing this, convince them that, with you as an ally, they are likely to win more often. They can get further with you than without you. Where possible, try to bring them into discussions on larger purposes, goals, and priorities. This can help move some of their backstage activities to front stage and create at least an island of trust. Gamesman are most often technically solid subordinates. Take advantage of their expertise and try to help them learn how to balance it by incorporating other decision criteria.

In the case of the Rebels, the danger for you as boss is letting their demonstrative style distract you from their value. Their contentiousness is usually harmless, and sometimes quite useful. Some bosses may view the Rebel's actions as a challenge to upper-level authority. This can lead to ill-advised attempts by you to reassert control. But since Rebels tend to be impatient and become easily frustrated, a more productive way to view them is as people who are merely testing their skill and exhibiting some impatience for more responsibility. It is also possible that they feel passion for the issues at hand and you are seeing their commitment to be involved.

Rebels are usually younger middle managers. While they struggle against structure and direction, their fight is most often over the means and methods to obtain largely acceptable outcomes. Take comfort in the fact that they usually buy into the overall goals and are arguing over better or best ways to get there. Self-esteem and confidence are very much at stake for the Rebels. Since Rebels have a low-distance orientation (more personal), you will find that acting the part of kindly uncle or aunt, and not taking their arguments personally, will get better results than assertions of managerial authority.

The Whistleblower has a very strong internal gyroscope that senses inappropriate or unethical behavior. Unlike the Rebel, this subordinate manager's problems with the organization go beyond conflicts over methods and concern basic goals and purposes. Conflicts with this subordinate are likely to involve much deeper questions than those that are raised by the Rebel. The Whistleblower's more withdrawn personal orientation makes it more difficult for both of you to negotiate difficulties.

The Whistleblowers, who are often technical experts, are constantly wary and vigilant for incongruities between what the organization professes to value, what you are directing them to do, and what they consider acceptable. They are more likely to see their ultimate responsibility to their profession or to society in general. Their organization's goals come next on their list of priorities, then their own personal sense of values. The boss's wishes tend to come last (unlike the Partisan, where they come first). Stay in good contact with Whistleblowers. They tend to be reluctant to express their views; by the time they come to you, the problem will be looming.

Whistleblowers do not need to be a problem as long as the organization and you are acting congruently. But their generally agreeable exterior (they are mostly deferential) masks a sharply defined set of convictions about what is right, proper, and congruent with larger values. For the ethical boss manager, they can be a useful sort of conscience and guide, alert to questionable behavior. The best option would be to take them into your confidence. Stay alert to and consider seriously any qualms they express about plans or activities.

For the boss manager inclined to cut corners, Whistleblowers may appear to go along, or go along for a while, until they become convinced that activities they are aware of, or are involved in, are wrong. They will then raise an alarm, going around or through you in order to have their concerns addressed. Ignoring, threatening, or dismissing their concerns will, in the final analysis, only make it worse for you, the boss.

The Boss's Role in Developing Flexibility in Subordinate Style

This book recommends that subordinate managers learn to become flexible in their approach to the boss-subordinate relationship. This adapting by subordinate managers needs to be complemented by adaptations from their bosses. Attempts to change organizational leadership styles have been hampered by the failure to address commensurate "followership" changes. Likewise, attempts to change subordinate approaches requires complementary changes by their bosses.

It is a partnership. It takes two. The failure to address this dooms many organizations to ineffective change processes. You cannot change the boss-subordinate relationship by changing the subordinate alone. The boss also has a role to play and will also be required to change to make the relationship effective.

Here are several recommendations for you as a boss. Even as you are making changes as a subordinate manager, you will need to think about doing these things in your relationship with your own subordinates.

Assess Your Managerial Style

Many bosses, like subordinates, have built-in reflexive responses to certain situations. I am often surprised by how many managers find it easy to describe their managerial style independent of the tasks they face. Many managers will assert they are participative or that they lean toward more autocratic methods. They make the error of thinking of their style as some innate quality of their person that ends up being applied across the board in all situations. They do not see it as a tool to be adjusted to the many different circumstances they face. As a result, they can fail to see that certain contrary responses from their subordinates are useful or appropriate.

Many managers, for example, are prone to see challenges from their subordinate managers as challenges to their own authority, competence, or personal expertise. Their reflexive reaction is to attempt to reassert control. Other bosses reflexively wait and check with subordinates before making decisions, even when decisive unilateral action may be what is most effective. These are the kinds of reflex responses that you as a boss need to learn to check yourself on. In short, what changes in your boss reactions must be made to complement the changes your subordinates are making?

As a boss, you need to develop a clear and preferably fact-based understanding of the facets of your own management style. How do you attempt to influence others? What is your learning style? Your communication style? Your approach to managing conflict? Do you tend to be autocratic in your decision making? Consultative? More group-centered? What assumptions do you hold about motivation? How do those assumptions fit with, or miss, your subordinates' interests and needs? The list could go on and on.

There are many useful assessment tools to help you gain some reliable views on these issues, and it is wise to use them. Your view about yourself is important, but try to find external sources of data to support, expand, and in some cases, contradict it. It is important that this self-assessment be accurate and consensually validated.

Managers find it tempting in the absence of information to make certain socially desirable assumptions about their managerial style. But as is the case in other arenas of human activity, how we see ourselves is often not how others see us. I may think I am principled and decisive. Someone else may see the same behavior as closed-minded and rigid. Remember, others' response to us is guided not by how we think we are, but how they think we are. If we will understand our relationships, we must find out how closely our self-perception aligns with others' perceptions of us.

When we discover how our behavior as managers might be "grooved," we can then learn how to complement our own preferences in the relationship with subordinates. Modern demands on organizations clearly suggest that managers and leaders learn to operate in multifaceted ways.

Organizational needs are changing along with the boss manager's role. I believe that there will always be a role for decisive, take-charge skills in managers. Not everything is, or should be, a group decision. They take more time and can be expensive as a strategy. Where expertise is concentrated in the minds of a few individuals, groups can reduce decision quality. Having acknowledged that, it also needs to be said that demands for innovation, quality, lowered costs, and leaner staffs are driving a need for more frequent use of empowering, bottom-up strategies. Boss managers need to operate less frequently from a fixed or preferred style and become more flexible and versatile.

Any grooved style you have operated from is likely to have

promoted a complementary or reactionary groove from your subordinates. If you have had an autocratic leaning, you may have inadvertently trained your subordinates to be seducers. Be alert to your own seduction by a subordinate who caters to your needs for control. He or she may be colluding with you in being ineffective.

If your task is a creative one, for example, being deferred to means you will not have two (or more) minds working on a problem. You will have one, your own. The subordinate manager will be trying to scope out what you want, so he can appear to support your ideas. It has been demonstrated that boss managers tend to rate highly, and get along better with, subordinate managers in the accommodating group. These are mostly high-deference and low-divergence subordinates.

The subordinate manager who takes issue with you, fights for a point of view, may be less easy for you to handle but might be providing you with a more valuable service. Watch out for your own negative emotional response. Other subordinates will read it (perhaps already have read it) and will be disinclined to support you through independent thought and pushing back.

Such subordinate contentiousness is not always best seen as a challenge of some sort. It may also indicate a higher state of readiness in the subordinates for more advanced responsibilities, an impatience to assume leadership. Their voice and the questions they raise can prompt rethinking by everyone and can ensure that all problem and solution sets are examined. Besides, in addition to promoting more careful analysis by everyone, the pushy ones (like Hal Sperlich and Lee Iacocca) may be right.

Be careful that any conflict that arises is focused on the task. If you like to be deferred to, challenge yourself to accept and reward managers who push back. You can, and probably should, insist that managers base their views in real data and reasoned analysis. Explain where you are trying to go, get agreement on overall targets, but open yourself as much as possible and support controversial viewpoints. Point out the weaknesses in your own arguments.

Explicitly and publicly thank those who raise contrary viewpoints to your own.

And, if you are a reflexive participator (or even a so-called abdicrat), consider that you may not provide enough structure for your subordinate managers or help promote their growth. In addition, you could be wasting valuable time when it is you who should be making the decision. Many managers who are uncomfortable with managerial authority welcome the current trends in autonomous teams and empowerment. However, they still need to exercise their authority when it is appropriate to do so. In those situations, boss managers should be decisive and directive. Subordinate managers used to offering input may need to just get their instructions and implement them. For many types of decisions, explaining your thought process afterward can serve to gain the commitment of subordinates just as well as their participation in the process of making the decision. Both parties adjust to the situational demands.

Assess the Tasks You and Your Subordinates Face

After you have developed an awareness of your own leanings as a manager, the next step is to begin to move from operating out of a set style toward operating in ways and relationship patterns that best serve the tasks at hand.

This means you must talk about these tasks with your subordinates; you will not be able to determine an appropriate relationship without having this kind of discussion. For most boss-subordinate pairs, many of the tasks that are faced can be predicted. Discuss those tasks and determine what is the best relationship strategy for each. Where does it make sense for your subordinate manager to operate in each of the different modes?

When the task requires a directive, telling approach by the boss (where the boss's expertise is obviously superior and decisive, the decision is structured, or it is a crisis demanding quick response), the subordinate manager is advised to operate in an accommodative mode. When the task is creative or innovative, the decision is not structured, and expertise or information is widely shared, then the boss-manager needs to flatten the authority structure and subordinate managers may need to push back more aggressively. When normal work is the priority, personalizing the relationship is less of a concern than when development is at issue or when the decision situation suggests managers clarify their respective value systems. When goals are in debate or mission is unclear, consider the issue of alignment.

Changing the way you relate to subordinates from task situation to task situation may be new for you and will probably be uncomfortable at first. But over time it will become natural.

Do not fall into the trap of meshing your styles so that you can be comfortable. Do not make comfort your highest priority. Effective work together may (and probably will) require both of you to be uncomfortable at least some of the time. Each of you will need to learn how sometimes to operate "out of style."

As an example, suppose you, as a boss, prefer to be in control in most situations and you have accommodating subordinate managers. A match? Yes. Comfortable? Probably. Effective? Not if you are charged with creative tasks, innovation, or some kind of organizational change. Or, on the other hand, suppose you are a participative manager with low-deference, autonomous subordinates who like to provide input. A match? Yes. Comfortable? Sure. Effective? Not in certain situations, such as those involving routine tasks, structured problems, or in some crisis situations. In these cases, this pair will likely suffer from several kinds of ineffectiveness: excessive time and delay making decisions, opportunity costs, higher decision-making costs, possible lower decision quality, and poor modeling of management behavior.

Most organizations these days are trying to innovate, raise quality, and keep costs down. You have fewer resources, including time. Even if you are prone to close management of your subordinate managers, new trends in organizing (like increased spans of control, and your broadened task responsibilities) will not allow you to indulge this preference. It suggests your subordinates will need to take more initiative and engage in more autonomous action within broad guidelines. This means you have to communicate goals and pathways to those goals to your subordinate managers. You provide resources, offer consultation, rely on them getting back to you, with agreed upon check-in and data reporting.

The subordinate managers who have adapted well to autocratic managerial styles and have come to require structure and guidance (accommodating styles) will certainly need to make substantial adjustments in these newer work situations. Autonomous managers need to make sure their efforts tie in to the work of others. And adversarial managers will need to temper and channel their impulses to achieve positive task results and reduce their own alienation.

Innovative tasks require certain kinds of interaction that are different from routine tasks, developmental tasks, or crisis situations. Figure out where these different kinds of tasks fit in your work together, and how you both might need to adapt. In this adaptation, consider subordinate manager readiness and expertise. Is training needed for either or both of you?

Identify arenas for pushing back and task situations where the subordinate manager needs to just make it happen. Decide when to discuss more personal, developmental matters. Discuss what goals you are trying to serve. Get agreement, or at least acknowledge divergence.

Divergence is a powerful force in this relationship. We know that when a boss-subordinate pair is out of alignment, disagreeing on goals or methods, they are often ineffective and waste energy. Alignment should consider goals first and then the methods used to achieve them. You can live with disagreement on methods, but not on goals. If the overall goals of the boss manager and the subordinate manager are at odds, resolve it before you try to get your work done.

Assess the Styles of Your Subordinates and Work Toward Flexibility

As a boss manager, you have considered your own preferences, particularly on the issues of control, making personal contact, and understanding and getting across overall goals to your subordinate managers. Next you have discussed with your subordinate managers what relationship approaches your tasks require. This discussion is an exchange of views; be careful not to announce or dictate what is required. Probe, ask, and listen. Remember that effective communication is two-way communication.

Now, have a discussion with your subordinates about their style. As we saw earlier, there are some general directions, given current organizational trends, for different subordinate styles to move to develop themselves. You can make this developmental interaction a regular part of performance appraisal, but I would recommend you do it more often than the periodic appraisal sessions.

What is your view of their leaning, their reflex? And how should that be rounded out? What is the subordinate's view of her style? Is it the same as your view? Reconcile any different views. The subordinate manager's view of herself should weigh heavily here. But it is important to develop a complex and consensual view.

I developed a version of the authority relations inventory (which forms the basis of this work) for bosses to fill out. In it, bosses answered questions based about how they saw their subordinate managers' style in relating to them. It was scored by the subordinate managers after they completed work on their own view of themselves. Most of the time there was significant difference on the deference scale. As mentioned earlier, most boss managers saw their subordinate managers as being more deferential (less pushy) than subordinate managers saw themselves. In the small group I studied, no systematic differences were apparent on the other two aspects of style.

Once you figure out a consensual view, both of you should discuss how and in what directions to round out the subordinate manager's flat sides.

Provide Feedback and Training

Subordinate styles are not easily changeable but they *can* change. And even if basic preferences do not change, subordinate managers can, with moderate effort and some help, learn how on a behavioral level to complement their preferred style with other approaches when those make sense. This change is all the more likely when you, their boss, are an active partner in the change process.

Such an adaptive competence is an achievable goal, but it requires some assistance and structure for practice and change. Getting accurate feedback on style and how the subordinate manager needs to develop are key first steps. Appreciating the general directions for change (becoming more adaptable, depending on task) as well as their personal directions (where do I, as a subordinate manager, start from?) are both important first tasks.

Next is some form of structured training. Training should be behaviorally based so that managers do not end up merely having learned a new language but little else. It is also important that managers be able to get direct personal feedback in this process. What is their individual orientation to the relationship with their bosses and how should they complement it to be more effective?

There also need to be structures that support change. The issue of the boss-subordinate relationship needs to be part of performance evaluation and the reward system as well. Conduct periodic debriefings with you as their manager and with competent, professional educators. Establish behavioral objectives for both parties to the relationship. Very little will result if it is left as an informal "let's do better" form of resolve.

Walk the Talk

Challenge yourself to implement these ideas in your daily behavior. This is what finally matters. Give yourself time to work into new relationship arrangements, but check from time to time whether you can see a difference. The purpose of this learning is to apply it, to have it make a discernible difference in how the relationship functions.

Any new behavior is likely to feel somewhat awkward and uncomfortable for a bit. That can be a sign that you are making progress.

Review, Reward, and Reevaluate

Make this deliberate and scheduled. Set aside time for a discussion. Get outside third-party assistance or use your human resources staff if you are not sure how to go about this. Look at the work you have been doing as a pair as well as your experience of your interactions. Return to specific exchanges to point to the things you have been doing well as well as the things that you have not been doing well.

Make sure you recognize and reward progress in changing the range of your interactions. Measure what you are doing against the behavioral objectives you created. Recognize change, and reward it with a compliment, a short letter to your subordinate manager and to the file, perhaps a lunch. Recognition does not need to be extravagant to have a very significant and positive motivational result.

Get feedback yourself and decide on effectiveness criteria that you will use with your managers in figuring out if you are working well together. Do not leave this criteria at "we seem to get along well." That does not always indicate you are being effective. Consider whether you want to stay on the course you have been on or make some adjustments in light of learning or new task demands.

Relationship structures should support your work, and as things change in your work, so should the relationship. Not all things can be foreseen, but reevaluate where you are heading.

Chapter Eight

Changing Authority Relations: Impacts on Organizational Processes

> It is important for me to advance in my current
> organization, and my organization rewards the good
> soldiers. There are times when I will not voice new
> ideas or argue a point of view because I don't want to
> be viewed as a rebel, not a team player. . . . They say
> one thing but reward another. How they expect to
> get innovation, to have people feel empowered, is
> beyond me.
>
> —*An executive in the research project*

This chapter deals with issues in the boss-subordinate relationship from an overall organizational perspective. Because it addresses many of the major change processes that organizations have taken on in recent times, processes that require or more readily yield to organization-level intervention, it is primarily intended for policy makers and others at the executive level.

Organizations today are embarked on many different kinds of change. Many of these changes are based on the idea that flatter, more organic, and adaptive team-based structures will be necessary for future organizational success. What are the implications of this kind of change for the boss-subordinate relationship? Will flatter organizations and team-based management mean that issues of authority relationships will gradually disappear? I do not think so.

At least three considerations support this conclusion. First, the changes toward completely new nonhierarchical forms will happen in only some kinds of organizations and are likely to take time, so that hierarchical forms will be around for a while in all organizations. Second, many organizations, while increasingly emphasizing team-based structures and flatter, more organic forms, will retain hierarchical structures; the focus in these organizations will be on improving such structures, not on sweeping them away. Finally, in either kind of organization, the ability to manage authority relationships will play a key role.[1]

The kinds of changes organizations are making take many forms:

- Increasing product or service quality
- Lowering costs
- Enhancing innovation and creativity
- Promoting employee empowerment
- Team-based management strategies (including self-managed or autonomous teams)
- More general employee self-guidance
- Reduced staff and downsizing
- Employee development and training for flexibility
- Breaking down cross-functional barriers to cooperation
- Changing upper-management roles and leadership styles
- Fostering commitment
- Developing greater strategic understanding throughout the organization
- Managing change
- Managing diversity and social justice
- Promoting more ethical individual and organizational behavior
- Developing greater cross-cultural competencies

The following sections will discuss some of the ways the issue of authority relationships, specifically the boss-subordinate relationship, will be important in achieving these changes. This is not to say that managing authority relationships is a panacea or some sort of silver bullet. The changes listed above represent complex interweavings of management practices, organizational structures, policies, goals, norms, and more. Many things must be addressed in order to bring about desired changes. But better management of authority relationships throughout the organization can play an important role.

The Starting Point

No matter what change effort your organization is engaged in, you need to ask: Who are the people you are asking to behave differently? From the perspective being offered in this book, this question of the target of change is answered by the three main groups of subordinate types. The accommodating, autonomous, and adversarial types will each respond to changes in the organization and in authority relationships in differing ways. We must therefore start with the fact that, in most organizations, there is a very large population of accommodating styles and smaller groups of autonomous and adversarial types.

Most organizations have been training and rewarding people in the accommodating styles for a long time. Subordinate managers with the autonomous styles have been more or less tolerated, while those with the adversarial style have often been punished. Although this pattern of relative values may have made sense in the past, this is no longer the case. If change along the lines outlined above is to come about, the accommodating types will need to become more independent, the autonomous styles will need more consistent support and rewards, and the adversarial styles will need to become more integrated into the organization.

In business and health care organizations, half of all managers are in the accommodating styles. This "good soldier" orientation, while potentially useful and certainly honorable, tends to rely too much on the guidance of authority to help in bringing about the changes many organizations are seeking. Managers operating with this approach, with their need for structure and guidance, will be frustrated in flatter, team-based cultures. These folks are not likely to have ready skills at independent or creative thinking and are not as likely as their autonomous or adversarial colleagues to push for ideas or to deliver vital (but unpopular) news and proposed solutions to their bosses. Their overall orientation to authority will lead these subordinates to respond to empowerment not as an opportunity (as the autonomous types will) but as a threat to their sense of structure and order in the organization. They are likely to voice skepticism and find ways to avoid true involvement.

Educational organizations, with their differing cultures and structures, face the reverse situation.[2] In these organizations, fewer managers use the accommodating approach (about one-third) while many more (two-thirds in all) operate in either the autonomous or the adversarial styles. The careful preservation and nurturing of individual prerogatives in these systems make developing consensus and focusing energies more difficult. People in such cultures tend to see requests for cooperation and more integrated functioning as unwarranted insults to strenuously acquired and maintained freedoms. As resources shrink, educational organizations and systems will be required to cut out less necessary functions and eliminate redundancies. This will require more people to operate in more interdependent ways. The autonomous and more adversarial types will need to learn how to become more collaborative and less independent.

Every type of organization, therefore, will need to carefully assess its overall culture with respect to the issue of authority relationships. What has been expected and rewarded in the past, and what are the new demands of the future? Following this, some groundwork will need to be laid by developing individual and cultural awareness of subordinate styles and the ways in which such styles can be adjusted for success.

In one of my consultations with a communications company, an upper-level manager explained to a large staff of engineers (most of whom had rated themselves, and had been rated by their bosses, into one or another of the accommodating styles) that with the demands of their business and the likelihood of reduced staff and increased spans of control, they would need to begin moving more toward the autonomous styles. Specific dimensions for development were isolated, and managers subsequently met with their boss managers for discussions and planning for development. With the help of their bosses and the support of upper levels, the subordinate managers made many significant changes; the upper-level managers reported that the culture of the staff group shifted noticeably.

Training programs, systems for communicating goals, the performance appraisal process, and reward systems will all need significant revamping. The direction of change in subordinate style will depend on the makeup of the subordinate group and how you and your organization have rewarded them and reinforced certain behaviors over others. In the case of business and health care organizations, more autonomous or more adversarial styles may be needed; in the case of many educational systems, more accommodative styles may need to be promoted.

General Effectiveness

In a recent study conducted by the St. Paul Fire and Marine Insurance Company (Beachy, 1992), a bad relationship with the boss was cited as the main cause of high worker stress by the twenty-eight thousand workers who participated in the study. Employees who said they had a poor relationship with the boss also reported low morale, higher absenteeism, and more stomach trouble. The study went on to point out that the characteristics of a good boss-subordinate relationship do not vary much, regardless of industry or rank in the organizational hierarchy.

Surprisingly, the study found that such stressors were more detrimental to job performance than some of life's worst traumas, including the death of a spouse or other close relatives. This was mainly because, for the latter, the employee could expect, and often receive, support from others as well as some eventual relief.

Another study reported the results of a survey of over one thousand college students on values important to them (Dyer and Dyer, 1984). Using the popular TV program M*A*S*H as a reference point for organizational values and processes, the study reported that one of the most desirable values espoused by the students was "being in an organization with superiors who interact with others because of their concern and desire to understand, and in which people treat others of lower rank or position with respect." Their first-ranked fear about their organizational future was "that I will find myself working under superiors who I will not respect or be able to follow with real commitment" (p. 72). The newer generation of organizational participants is, rightfully, very concerned with this relationship.[3]

Divergence and the Climate of Self-Protection

Changes toward flatter structures depending on more participative management will not get very far until top-management teams can reduce or, better yet, remove the climate of fear that pervades many organizations, both large and small. When subordinates at any level are primarily concerned with their self-protection, real and honest dialogue becomes impossible, creativity suffers, people resist pushing their management teams for necessary and appropriate changes, and bad news is either distorted and not delivered at all.

The most powerful of the three dimensions I have discussed in this book is divergence. Remember that, as divergence increases, the quality of the relationship between bosses and subordinates declines. The question here involves the alignment between bosses and subordinates over the goals their work seeks to make real and the methods they use to achieve those goals. When bosses and subordinate are out of phase with each other, or in clear disagreement, little of permanence can be accomplished. Game playing, politics, sabotage, and adversarial relating become commonplace.

This suggests that all organizations need to put a lot of energy into communicating goals of the overall organization, the subunit, and the individual. Further, organizations need to bring everyone into dialogue over goals, organizational mission, and values. It is not enough to merely post these things on bulletin boards or to do some one-way communication in large meetings. Forms of organizational communication and discussion should allow and encourage real two-way communication. Buy-in by everyone in the organization into basic goals and methods should be a top priority, even if outside help is needed to get productive discussions going. If people do not understand and accept where they are heading, and how they are supposed to get there, they cannot function even semiautonomously.

Once this dialogue has started, the language of organizational goals and values needs to be integrated into performance appraisal forms and processes. If you say you want quality, get agreement on this, specify what it means, specify how people's individual behavior contributes to or detracts from quality, and then evaluate (and reward) people on their contribution to this goal.

Increasing Quality

In the quest to increase product or service quality, organizations depend on the willingness of people at all levels to apply their operations knowledge and general creativity to solve problems and suggest improvements. But this by itself will do little if people are not rewarded (or worse, are punished) for asserting their knowledge upward, for faithfully and promptly transmitting ideas and information to superiors, even bad news, and for being willing to tell the boss that he or she is wrong.

Even the notorious John R. "Neutron Jack" Welch of General Electric has asserted, "We cannot afford management styles that suppress and intimidate . . . managers must be open to ideas from anywhere. . . . It is embarrassing to reflect that for probably 80 or 90 years, we've been dictating equipment needs and managing people who knew how to do things much faster and better than we did" (Holusha, 1992). With his clarion call for major changes at GE, Welch has been encouraging communication outside traditional channels and promoting widespread participation by lower-level employees in decision making.

One of the relevant findings in the research reported in this book is that managers typically think of themselves as pushing harder for influence than their bosses think they do. The subordinate manager commonly thinks he has disagreed vociferously with the boss, while the boss typically hears only a tepid response and not much attempt at influence. This disparity in perception suggests that in many relationships, subordinate managers can afford to be more energetic in their "push back" (and perhaps boss managers might do better to listen more carefully). To gain this involvement, boss managers must do more than indicate a wish for it or an openness to it. They must model it and then reward it.

Innovation and Creativity

These are much-discussed topics these days. Peters and Waterman, in their book *In Search of Excellence* (1982), talked about the key role in innovation of the product champions, "those individuals who believe so strongly in their ideas that they take it on themselves to damn the bureaucracy and maneuver their projects through the system" (p. xviii). They go on to note the key role in excellent companies of "small competitive bands of pragmatic bureaucracy-beaters, the source of much innovation" (p. xviii).

Such "antibureaucrats" are chiefly defined by their resistance to conformity, the refusal to follow the company line, their reluctance to adopt the view of the hierarchy, and a willingness to go against established authority for the good of the organization and for their own personal sense of achievement. Organizations filled with, and rewarding, accommodating types can expect little of this.

To re-create the entrepreneurial spirit in organizations, Tom Peters (1988, 1994) also advocates a minimalist headquarters, business units "owned" by the customers, knowledge workers who consider themselves professional providers of services, and individualism. "Hire the anarchist!" says Peters. "The only way to have interesting stuff going on is to have crazy men and women running parts of your organization! . . . Be malcontents, system evaders and beaters who constantly push the limits . . . push against the way it's always been done and those who promote the status quo."

We have been attempting for some time now to change management roles and leadership styles. In general, we have been seeking to change managers toward being more like coaches, resource providers, and facilitators.

While we attempt these changes to boss managers, it is also necessary to address the commensurate changes demanded of those in subordinate roles. "Organizations stand or fall partly on the basis of how well their leaders lead, but partly also on the basis of how well their followers follow" (Kelley, 1988, p. 142). If these changes are to be effective and permanent, both parties to the relation must move appropriately.

An article in *Business Week* described the efforts of president John Smith of General Motors to shake up GM's "hierarchical and fiefdom-clogged bureaucracy" (Kerwin, Treece, and Schiller, 1992). It described Smith's creation of an "inner circle," a strategy board, to assist him in getting GM back to profitability. It was described as an unusual group, which "includes newcomers who are willing to challenge assumptions and bash bureaucracy." It is a sad comment that many organizations are having to go outside to obtain staff with the capacity and willingness to push their bosses *and* the system.

Divergence is an engine for creativity, yet many organizations may be choking off creativity in top-management ranks. This conclusion is based on one of the other striking findings of this research: As managers move up in the organization there is a significant decrease in their sense of divergence. This means that, as managers become more senior, they increasingly buy in to the goals of the upper-management groups that they enter. A troubling implication of this is that conformity is the price to be paid for admission to higher levels.

Given the tendency of most organizations to reward the accommodating styles, this seems probable. Top managers tend to select into their own ranks people who think and act like they do, people who have been amenable to top-management control and direction. Expecting creative thinking based on divergent views from such managers contradicts the essentially accommodative conditioning and reinforcement they have been through.

What all this means is that among those who have influence, who decide on allocations of resources and overall directions, there is little impetus to think differently. These top-management teams tend to agree on and to reinforce past decisions and decision makers. They will often develop a striking and seamless unanimity (even to developing a fortress mentality) in rejecting proposals that differ from their own prevailing views.

Those who do think differently, those bureaucracy beaters, who are higher on divergence (like the Rebels), are typically younger and newer and found at lower levels without the authority to do much about or with their ideas. Others, such as the Gamesmen, Whistleblowers, and Independents, who could be relied on for some independent thought and creativity, tend to be more marginal and found in the lower-power, and lower-level, staff groups. Their style as a sort of organizational irritant often results in their being uninfluential and not often promoted.

Further, many of these subordinate managers are women, whose continuing exclusion from the higher levels is well documented.

Expecting them to move innovative ideas through management layers of self-protective accommodators is expecting too much. It is not likely to happen with any consistency.

The implications for innovation in organizations when product and service life cycles have become dramatically shortened should not be underestimated. Much more rapid and effective movement of ideas to markets has to be made. Top-management groups who value innovation and creativity need to link these more divergent individuals directly to decision makers with the authority and autonomy to act on new ideas in timely ways.

There is a warning here for many organizations that must innovate to survive. Continuing to place a high value on responsiveness and obedience to formal authority may doom the organization to extinction. Mark Reutter (1988) describes how in the operations at Bethlehem Steel, the former giant, no superintendents or managers ever dared question or challenge their company's sixty-year-old operating methods and practices. It was a culture that dismissed new ideas, spurned product research, choked off innovation and innovators, and brushed aside new technologies.

Top management and the board of directors at Bethlehem Steel was made up only from insiders, most of whom who had worked their way up in the company. Few managers were ever hired from outside. Everyone throughout the organization catered to the beliefs of the conservative main office and, when called upon, parroted the views of top management, whose ranks they hoped to join. Even when Bethlehem Steel had gone from ninth place on Fortune's 500 in 1957 on to eighty-ninth place in 1986, the new chairman, Walter Williams, described as a long-time company man, stated to reporters for the New York Times "that he would apply no new philosophies in his efforts to restore profitability" (Reutter, 1988, p. 82). Like those before him, years of socialization to a way of thinking had taken a toll. He simply could not think any other way. Reutter concludes, "Such was the hazard of a corporate culture that had rewarded conformity and promoted insiders" (p. 77).

Business, health care, government, and the military are all relatively high-deference, low-divergence cultures. Given that all these institutions are being pressed to make transforming changes, such a composition does not augur well for their capacity to reinvent, reengineer, or reform themselves in any way without systematically addressing the cultures of status quo and risk aversion.

The nonaccommodating styles, so crucial to this kind of change, clearly feel the least support from their bosses, the lowest concern by their bosses for their careers, and the greatest need for self-protection. The Rebels, Gamesmen, Whistleblowers, and Independents offer organizations the greatest potential for innovative ideas. Yet they are likely to be the most estranged from the organizational mainstream and be negatively evaluated. They are the least likely to get sponsored by their bosses and the least likely to stay with their organizations.

Reduced Staff and Downsizing

Over the last thirty years, the number of people in management as a percentage of all employees has ballooned because of management approaches to control, monitoring, and oversight. This has left many organizations with much higher cost structures than can be sustained in the global marketplace. Now we are seeing many organizations reducing staff and becoming leaner. If organizations are to stay cost competitive, they will need to alter not only their approaches to managing (leading) but also their approaches to authority relationships.

Because of this reduction in staff, managers at all levels are likely to have increased spans of control and responsibility. Sheer force of numbers and workload will require that their subordinate managers be more self-starting, risk-taking, decision-making, and autonomous. More traditional approaches to managing and being a subordinate will need to yield. Such trends are further reinforced by the movement to empower people at all levels.

We need to develop more autonomy and self-guidance within a well-articulated, well-communicated, and agreed-on goal structure. In addition, organizations must now rely on subordinate managers, at all levels, to bring their bosses into play at the right times and to manage horizontal relationships (across functions) without the mediation of higher levels of authority.

Empowerment and Participation in Decision Making

A few years ago, I approached a large insurance company whose top managers had expressed an interest in participating in my research. I was surprised to learn when I arrived that this interest was not shared by their manager of human resources. She told me in no uncertain terms that she was interested in empowering her organization's managers; she did not want them focusing on their relationship to authority.

I was dumbfounded by her assertion; how can you do one without the other? To me empowerment means more than just boss managers doing some things differently. Subordinate managers also need to refashion their approach to their relationship to authority. For true empowerment to happen, both parties to the relationship need to change. In fact, it seems to me that empowering is fundamentally about changing the relationship to authority away from dependence and passivity and oversight toward more partnership, autonomy, risk taking, and negotiated roles. This is not solely the work of higher-powered members of the relationship.

Many other management consultants and researchers are advocating fundamental changes in the way relationships are structured and operating in organizations. They, like Peters, are promoting a new form of decentralization and empowering workers at all levels of the organization. While it is tempting to see such change as changing approaches to leadership and management (the popular downward view), it is clear that the relations subordinates pursue with their bosses must also change. The proposed sort of joint decision making that is often referred to as empowerment will go nowhere if bosses and subordinates together are unable to alter the fundamental premises and distinctions that have characterized this relationship in the past.

Geert Hofstede ([1980] 1991b), an acclaimed international management researcher, writes, "Whatever a naive literature on leadership may give us to understand, leaders cannot choose their styles at will; what is feasible depends to a large extent on the cultural conditioning of a leader's subordinates" (p. 361).

Both parties to this key relationship will have to do new things. It takes two.

An analysis of the Air Florida crash into the Potomac River in Washington, D.C., in 1982 revealed that the cause was twofold: pilot misinterpretation of data *and* the first officer's failure to press home to the pilot information he had about inadequate thrust for takeoff. Only five people survived this accident. While numerous references were made to pilot error, like many such accidents it can more accurately be attributed to a relationship failure. In a BBC documentary entitled "The Wrong Stuff," the filmmakers observed that it was as if the copilot would rather die than violate assumptions and tradition about challenging someone in a position of authority.

One way organizations can help is through addressing this important relationship in training and development efforts. As the experience of Chris, an airline pilot, illustrates, it can have an important effect: "As cockpit resource management [CRM] training began to emphasize crew members asserting their disagreement with the captain, I found myself experiencing internal conflict due to my authority relationships perceptions. I did overcome my hesitations in this regard. I subsequently had two occasions in which I was compelled to physically take control of the aircraft to avert a problem. To this day, I am not sure I would have done so, had I not been exposed to CRM, and accepted the premise that I could legitimately assert disagreement with the captain."

Team-Based Management

These team strategies are closely related to pushing authority down-ward in organizations. Managers who have been accustomed to top-down decision making are likely to find the idea of giving substantial decision-making authority to teams more than a bit uncomfortable and confusing.

Certain types of subordinates (autonomous styles) will operate well within these more fluid structures, but other types (such as the accommodating styles) are likely to feel lost. Their conception of their roles and their orientation to personal responsibility are likely to be sorely tried in these arrangements. As a result, without some support for change, they are likely to add little value to these efforts, at least in the short term.

The more adversarial styles will be useful in these activities, par-ticularly change initiatives, but will require adept handling by their peers and higher-level managers. They, along with their auton-omous colleagues, like the freedom teams provide, but they are not adept at developing horizontal synergies. They are more accustomed to independence or marginal positions or both. Accommodating styles, on the other hand, are accustomed to having these cross-functional relationships mediated by the boss. Doing it face to face will be a big change for those who prefer familiar structures.

As teams are expected to more directly manage cross-functional relationships, upper-level managers need to recognize that many managers have been accustomed to having these relationships mediated by organizational authority, usually their bosses. Devel-oping advanced conflict-management skills in these teams should therefore be a priority.

Employee Development: Training for Flexibility, Selection, and Promotion

Part of all managers' development needs to include gaining an understanding of their subordinate style and its strengths and weaknesses. As we have seen, subordinate style affects managers' ability to get resources from higher-level managers, to gain access to information, and many aspects of performance measured in performance reviews.

It has also been demonstrated that the amount of influence managers have with their subordinates is directly related to how much influence they have with the boss. It is as much a part of management style as the approach to leadership and needs attention in learning situations. It is appropriate that this is made a part of employee development training.

Upper-level managers should consider this facet of style as much as any other in their choices for promotions and for other assignments. Raising it for explicit attention will help boss managers establish more effective mentoring relationships. It will also improve selection processes by helping to create and maintain more appropriate mixes of accommodating, autonomous, and adversarial styles at all levels. As we have already discussed, continued reflexive promotion of the more accommodating styles will exacerbate problems in such areas as creativity, innovation, ethics, and strategy formulation—to name just a few.

Managing Change

As we have begun to realize that change is not merely an episodic event, we are coming to realize that managing change is not an occasional challenge but a permanent condition, a fact of organizational life. One author referred to it as "permanent whitewater" (Vaill, 1989). In this more rapidly changing world, authority-driven structures are too slow to change. Where organizations adopt a top-down model for management and socialize their managers at all levels to carefully observe the chain of command, quick adaptive responses to changing conditions are not likely to happen. Organizations will need to adapt and probably become a bit more chaotic in the process.

One group of prominent researchers and experts on corporate renewal commented, "In effect, companies are moving from the hierarchical and bureaucratic model of organization that has characterized corporations since World War II to what we call the task driven organization where what has to be done governs who works with whom and who leads" (Beer, Eisenstat, and Spector, 1990, p. 158).

With well-trained management groups, operating with their own discretion and within the broad guidelines established higher up, organizations can be nimble and effective. But this means helping such managers move out of their customary ways of relating to their bosses and others in positions of authority.

Beer and colleagues found that in successful corporate renewal and transformation, managers did not wait for senior management to start the process. They did not wait passively for a push from the top, or even in many cases an okay from the top. Rather, these managers initiated successful innovation and change themselves and *then* looked to top management to help diffuse the change throughout the organization and to create supportive structures and policies to help sustain the changes.

Ethical Behavior

Organizational and managerial ethics has been getting a great deal of attention recently because of a bewildering and frightening display of illegal and immoral acts. It is clear that organizations need to operate with a more fundamental and balanced regard for their larger physical, social, moral, and cultural environments.

Two researchers, in a book entitled *Crimes of Obedience*, discuss larger social and organizational processes that create, allow, and sustain crimes of obedience (Kelman and Hamilton, 1989). They are: *authorization*, where the individual is absolved of the responsibility to make personal moral choices; *routinization*, which organizes the action so that there is no opportunity to raise moral questions; and *dehumanization*, the structuring of attitudes so that it is neither necessary nor possible to see the relationship in moral terms; the victims are deprived of identity and community. The authors argue that it is through these processes that the average person becomes capable of dispassionate and obedient execution of policies that are morally repugnant and perhaps illegal.

Organizations are fertile ground for this pattern of behavior because organizations naturally diffuse responsibility. It is often hard to determine or reconstruct exactly who proposed or initiated some action. This is because it may have been the product of more than one mind or because, through successive interpretations of proposals, no one recognizes it anymore, has followed through on its execution or its source, or is willing to claim it. Origination, then, is often unclear, but those in implementation roles assume that someone in top management has authorized the proposal.

Organizations have numerous mechanisms to sustain and regularize actions while severing them from personal agency. Something can become standard operating procedure without anyone intending it. Someone in a subordinate role can easily assume, decide, or be told (with or without real authority): this is what "they" (higher-level authority) want. Given the accommodating nature of most organizational participants, such action is likely to be repeated until and unless someone with authority directs it to stop. The people who are implementing the directive are not likely to consider it their "own" and will rarely assume a personal responsibility for the ultimate outcomes. They will often not know, or perhaps not wish to know, the reason behind it (if there is one). Those higher up in the organization may not even be aware of the actions that are occurring under their presumed sponsorship.

I am reminded of a former client, an assistant plant manager, who decided to find out if the fourteen reports he was "required" to issue each month were really necessary, as they represented a debilitating regular additional workload. He took a bold step: he stopped issuing every one of them and waited to see if anyone would notice.

After three months, he had received calls on only four reports. In one case, divisional authorities called to thank him for cutting back their paperwork. They claimed they had never wanted the report in the first place. In another case, it turned out that the original request was for a one-time report, not a repetitive one. The original request went back several years to a divisional manager who was no longer with the company; his replacement claimed he never wanted the report and did not understand it but figured somebody else must have wanted it since it continued. No one did. The manager now issues three monthly reports.

With the common organizational characteristics of large size (making communications both mediated through layers and difficult), impersonal interaction patterns (where feelings about and reactions to activities are not likely to be raised), and narrowly defined functional loyalties (where few can see the ultimate effects of their part of the action), organizations can be massively destructive while few are aware and fewer still, or even no one, assumes responsibility for the damage.

While some argue that organizations should be bound to some fixed standard or ideal of ethical principles, this is not likely to be effective. It is not that codes of ethics are not worthy, but they have been around a long time and do not seem to have the desired effect. It seems more promising to articulate and utilize the moral diversity that exists within every social system but is often rendered silent through the weight of organizational authority structures.[4]

Within every organization are multiple value systems and varying perspectives on the organization's rights, duties, and responsibilities. These value systems in all their diversity can help to energize the organization's moral gyroscope and keep it from committing acts against the society it is intended to serve. We have known for a long time that organizational participants differ in their views of their organizations depending on where they reside in the structure.

In a fascinating discussion of how groups and organizations

produce extreme behavior and violence, one researcher cites as a primary cause the reduction of "normative dissonance" (Mills, 1982, p. 78). Using the Jonestown debacle as an example, the author specifies how complete commitment to a goal (low divergence) and high deference to authority dampen and inhibit "the interplay of complex and partially inconsistent norms and values of the group and its environment" (p. 78).

This interplay of differing views and value systems promotes questioning of actions and reconsideration of moral premises for behavior. These processes generally support more ethical conduct. In short, I am much more likely to question the rightness of my thinking and behavior when there is someone who disagrees with me and (this is important) is free to voice the disagreement. This interplay of differing views is what helps social systems (including organizations) maintain a moral center.

When such interplay is made difficult, reduced, or even eliminated through selective membership, socialization, barriers to communication, or simple prohibition by authority punishing questioners, awareness of divergence and different ways of looking at and valuing things tend to disappear. Mills concludes that the "loss of this damping process leads to a kind of supercommitment in which autonomy, both in moral judgement and role behavior, is replaced by unquestioning obedience, even to participation in violence" (p. 78).

Unfortunately, traditional organizations quite naturally do a number of the things that suppress awareness and consideration of moral divergence. It is important within organizational systems that cross-level dialogue be created, expanded, and sustained to incorporate as many of these diverse elements as possible. Many of the subordinate styles within the autonomous and adversarial categories maintain independent and even contrary views to those that commonly prevail in their organizations. It is the responsibility of upper management in these organizations, as a regular part of managing, to see that these individuals and views are brought into decision-making processes.

Managing Diversity and Social Justice

Men and women approach authority relationships differently. However, in stating this, I must quickly add that I do not believe that this is an inherent and permanent product of biological differences. Rather, these differences are much more likely to be the result of culture and learning and are therefore changeable for both men and women. Bear in mind that while the statements below are generally true and supported by statistical evidence, they are not universally true. Many women (as well as any specific woman) may feel differently.

The differences between men and women on the issue of deference are striking and have consequences for their participation in organizations, their developmental agendas, and how their managers relate to them. In general, women are much more insistent than men on reducing the power gap between themselves and their bosses to a minimum. They express stronger discomfort with the symbols and trappings of authority and are likely to notice, and dislike, attempts by their bosses to surround themselves with signs of class distinction. Bosses, in their eyes, not only have an obligation to consult with subordinate managers but they should also be receptive to and heed the advice of subordinates.

This suggests that managers who observe the forms of participative and empowering approaches (asking for input) but not the substance (opening themselves to influence) are likely to get a much stronger negative reaction from women than men. While this style orientation (low deference) is generally needed in organizations, it is rarely rewarded. And it appears that this push for influence has larger negative consequences for women with their bosses than for men who do likewise.

Contrary to popular stereotypes of women managers as being more attuned to relational skills, to a sense of community, and to personal rather than role relating, it appears that with their bosses this is not the case. In my research there are no overall differences between men and women on the distance scale. Women, on the whole, show no markedly different preference for personal relating over role relating with their bosses. There are no differences between the percentage of women who indicate a preference for a role relationship with their bosses and the men who indicate likewise. Similarly, there is no difference between the percentage of women and men who indicate a preference for a more personal relationship with their bosses.

But there are some differences between men and women with respect to distance when we look more closely at some of the details of distance orientation. For example, women believe more strongly than men that subordinate managers *should* establish more personal contact with their bosses and that contact between bosses and subordinates should not be limited to work-related matters. This desire makes sense particularly for developmental purposes and the creation of mentoring relationships.

However, women also report a quite striking and opposing need: the dramatic difference in their felt need for self-protection in the relationship with their bosses and their resistance to self-disclosure as a means of personalizing relationships.

It begins to become clear why women show a preference for the autonomous styles. These styles place them apart from authority and help to assuage their concerns about entangling themselves with organizational authority. However, this fear also results in the loss of developmental interactions (an appropriate form of work intimacy) and in certain instances means they must work without sufficient connection to or awareness of the goals they are serving.

The result of this pattern of low deference, high distance, and sometimes high divergence can easily be a form of marginality. While this preference exists to varying degrees for women, if we were to extend each preference to its extreme, it turns out to be the base pattern for the Gamesman style, one that reports the poorest relationships with those in authority. This marginal leaning for women is partly induced by their bosses and their organization, and partly by women's response to them.

Within any style pattern women consistently report poorer relationships with their bosses than men do. When it is an "approved" style, one that is typically rewarded in organizations, women report fewer positive results. Where it is patterns of behavior that are rewarded, women managers report getting along less well (not badly) with their bosses than men do. There appears to be less reward for being the stereotypical "good citizen" when the subordinate manager is a woman. When it comes to patterns of behavior that are not rewarded or even punished in organizations, women managers report much worse relationships than their male counterparts who behave similarly. Women who push their bosses for influence report much worse relationships than men who do likewise.

It appears there are greater risks for women in taking a more distant orientation (less personal) with their bosses if they are going to push for influence. For men who push their bosses (are low on deference), it appears to make little difference to the quality of their relationships whether they push from a role orientation or a more personal one. However, it seems that if a woman manager is going to push her bosses for influence, to maintain good relationship quality, she had better do it from a more personalized sort of relationship.

It is troubling to note that bosses appear much less willing to accept a woman who is pressing to have influence in decision making, especially if she is operating from a role orientation. It may well be that there is some transfer of expectations from the social arena into the work arena on the part of organizational authority for how women should behave. It is probable that male managers' performance evaluations of women subordinates are unduly influenced by these expectations.

This creates a bind for women who express (well-founded) concerns about bosses not being very adept at distinguishing developmental or work intimacies from other, inappropriate, intimacies. Women's fears about harassment and discrimination understandably provoke self-protective responses and force a sort of personal withdrawal. Yet as they try to have an impact from a role orientation, their bosses seem to respond much more negatively than they do to men managers who behave similarly. Women, in their need for self-protection, are forced into a pattern of exchange that seems to arouse their bosses' ire, and thereby diminishes their influence and their chances for mentoring and sponsorship, promotions, and the like.

These findings reinforce and support the idea that male managers need careful training in distinguishing (in behavioral terms) these intimacies. What are appropriate developmental and task-related intimacies and how are they different than inappropriate intimacies? One noted study of sexual harassment at the University of Pennsylvania defined it as the confluence of authority relations and sexual interest (Benson and Thompson, 1983). While the offense begins with the inappropriate advances of the party to the relationship with the higher power (who is usually male), such instances also reveal a confusion on the part of women about appropriate ways to relate to organizational authority. This is not to suggest that women are at fault. It is to say that women need to develop skills at managing themselves in the authority relationship so that they can more effectively meet the career challenges posed for them by participation in large organizations.

Top-management teams also need to create cultures where people of either gender are free from devoting a lot of energy to self-protection. Organizations are desperately in need of cultivating the skills that the more autonomous styles (preferred styles for women) have already developed. While women need to learn more integrative skills and be more willing to co-manage the necessary personal forms of relating with bosses, it is unrealistic to expect them to do so in a climate of threat.

Top-level executives must realize and accept that organizational cultures have subtly and powerfully woven into their fabric shared, and usually unstated, discriminatory expectations and criteria. It is no surprise that women in the managerial ranks are opting out of participation in large-scale systems in droves, choosing their own entrepreneurial ventures where they can create new rules and succeed or fail based on their merits and skills, not their gender.

Organizational leadership must recognize not only the issues of social justice but also the important role that diversity of all kinds plays in several vital organizational processes (such as innovation, creativity, and ethics). Careful review of promotion systems, criteria (stated and unstated), and personal reactions (conscious and unconscious) needs to be done. More important than whether someone personally likes or dislikes a certain style, or whether it violates someone's expectations of how any subgroup should behave, is the question of how well the style supports the task the organization is asking the individual to do. And, if it does not, the organization has a responsibility to assist the individual to realize this and learn other, more adaptive responses.

International and Cross-Cultural Competencies

Organizations today are concerned as never before with the cross-cultural aspects of managing. There are many things that are affected as we move across national and cultural boundaries. One of the most obvious differences is how people at all levels of the organization relate to organizational authority and the expectations they have for those functioning in those roles.

Such changes are most evident in the movement of former socialist or communist economies to market systems. It is a daunting change for those who have been trained for generations to take orders and implement them, to be passive and risk averse, to now move toward more self-directed and self-guided operations. Learning to assert one's opinions to a boss and push for operating changes will take time and require negotiating whole new systems of authority relationships and supporting organizational structures.

Regrettably, in this research project, there is not yet a large enough sample to make supportable statements on this important issue. But other people's work has touched on this dimension.[5] They strongly support the idea that as boss managers move across cultures, they must be alert to the widely varying expectations on the part of subordinate managers for how bosses will function and the ways in which subordinate managers will relate to them.

A good example involves participation in decision making. In the United States, managers who extend opportunities to participate in decision making to their subordinate managers are considered enlightened. In other cultures, such an act is tantamount to admitting ignorance and an inappropriate uncertainty. It is likely to bring about loss of respect and confidence. Boss managers in many cultures are expected to have (and demonstrate) greater expertise than their subordinates, and such invitations can alarm lower-level managers and engender feelings of insecurity.

From the subordinate's perspective, how a subordinate handles a relationship with an American boss is going to be different from how one handles a relationship with a Japanese, or German, or French boss. The acceptability or nonacceptability of subordinates operating outside the hierarchy is viewed quite differently from culture to culture. Particularly in matters of initiative, deference, and managing personal distance, subordinates will need to carefully attend to cross-cultural variations.

These differences do not imply that managers simply accommodate these expectations. From the standpoint of task accomplishment, other more stratified cultures will need to do some changing in their expectations and norms for organizational behavior. Organizational worlds and technology make it impossible for any one person to master all the knowledge that he or she must be concerned with. Managers from other cultures will need to begin changing their expectations for how people in authority will function, much as the highly individualistic U.S. culture is having to how to learn to operate in teams.

This does suggest that, as managers move across cultures, they should be aware when their actions are contradicting cultural norms and expectations. Special explanations and training will be quite useful whether managers are called upon to manage others in a different culture or are in the increasingly common position of being managed by a boss from another culture.

Appendixes

This section is divided into four parts. The first lays out the values and aspirations that guided this inquiry. The second spells out the method that evolved from those values and aspirations. The third part contains the statistical analysis of the research questionnaire and the self-assessment inventory. The fourth presents some interesting findings and reasoned speculation from smaller, related investigations.

A. Aspirations in the Development of a Theory

I have always been interested in the effects of leadership on organizations, the power of those in subordinate roles, and the effects of organizations on society. Related to these interests is the issue of how those in subordinate roles can help make their leadership more competent and effective.

Organizations can be and often are incredible amplifiers of the values and actions of relatively tiny constituencies and even individuals. They are remarkably effective at extending the reach of these individuals and small groups throughout a society and even around the globe. When an organization and its leadership are engaged in worthwhile activities, this characteristic works to everyone's benefit. When their ends are foolish, ill considered, dangerous, or even evil, this characteristic makes such instruments truly frightening.

In recent years, we have seen quite a few examples of resistance to change, inept or foolish choices, and policies promoted by small, insulated leadership cliques in organizations. Such organizations have, in many instances, fallen on hard times and been met with dramatically declining fortunes or even outright failure. Results include loss of jobs and far-reaching effects on society in general. In addition to these examples of bad or delayed decisions, there have been many acts of organizational malfeasance. People now tend to mistrust organizations and their regard for the societal welfare. The whistleblower has become something of a cultural icon.

When we have witnessed unfortunate, distressing, or even frightening outcomes, our reactions seem almost predictable. We search for *someone* to be responsible and take the blame. Perhaps we can point the finger at some inept, immoral, crazy, or evil leader. And undoubtedly there is a great deal of the blame that should often be apportioned to such "leadership." Sometimes, in addition to, or instead of, the leader, we seek some other person to be responsible. It is perhaps part of the cultural wiring in the United States that we are given to think in terms of individuals and individual responsibility.

Leadership and Followership

But what we tend to ignore is that the beliefs, views, and actions of any individual, including those in leadership roles, can have little effect if those things are not made real, amplified, and extended through the actions of those in follower or subordinate roles. And by this, I do not mean only the people at the lowest levels of the organization. I also include subordinates at all layers of management—from upper-level through midlevel to lower-level management as well. It is this group who must be engaged, directed, maneuvered, or manipulated into support for a leader. Whether their accommodation to authority is energetic (going above and beyond the call), conscientious (do exactly what is required), or even passive and indifferent (do not obstruct), things begin to happen on a large scale.

Kelman and Hamilton (1989) labeled this behavior "crimes of obedience." What these instances of social and organizational wrongdoing all have in common is poor, flawed, or even insane leadership *coupled* to scores of accommodating subordinates or followers. Without these subordinates and followers, and their willingness to at least go along (if not lend their creativity to initiatives), little could happen. As one author put it, "Without his armies, after all, Napoleon was just a man with grandiose ambitions" (Kelley, 1988, p.142). And these subordinates do not need to be evil or malicious people. The vast majority are not; they are ordinary people with common capacities, a wish for inclusion, and a desire to be conscientious about their jobs. In most situations, these are positive attributes and they are often rewarded by organizations.

False Comfort

It seems more comforting when we are trying to understand events if we can find at least some of these people to be incompetent or even monsters, but evidence supports the argument that these agents are, for the most part, just normal people. Like the subjects in the Milgram experiments in obedience (Milgram, 1974) or the prison guards in the Stanford prison studies (Zimbardo, 1973), they are average people with, in most contexts, acceptable values.

However, once in the organizational context, these normal qualities (wish to be included, be cooperative, feel valued, be a member of the team) can be exploited. This can easily result in dangers to the individual, the organization, and society in general. Their accommodating orientation to their role as subordinate participants is combined with several very common characteristics of organizations. These characteristics include the diffusion of responsibility, unclear origins for initiatives, and a blindness to the outcomes of collective actions. The results can be disastrous.

For example, after teams of psychiatrists examined Adolf Eichmann, Hitler's deputy in charge of the deportation machinery, they found him to be mild-mannered, average, normal. As one doctor put it, he seemed "saner than I am after having examined him" (Arendt, 1963, p. 22). Instead of finding the monster he was thought to be, they found he harbored no hatred of Jews. He felt to the end that he had only (and always) done his duty and had not harmed anyone. Instead of political zealotry, they found his main worries as he anticipated the fall of the Third Reich were the loss of a place to belong to and the absence of structure it would bring about in his daily life. Arendt commented, "It would have been very comforting indeed to believe that Eichmann was a monster. . . . The trouble . . . was that so many were like him—neither perverted nor sadistic. . . . They were and still are terribly and terrifyingly normal" (p. 253).

As Milgram discovered (in his famous obedience studies at Yale in 1974), there is an amazing capacity in all men (and women) to go along with what they perceive as, or can be convinced is, a legitimate authority. It is this capacity married to some of the common characteristics of organization that merits our individual and collective vigilance. Without the willingness to go along, in the absence of the accommodative behavior toward authority, the dangers faced by society from this source would, I believe, be greatly diminished. Long after the Second World War, one researcher wrote, "Many in the psychoanalytic mode were not unduly puzzled by the behavior of Hitler and other Nazi leaders—that could be understood in orthodox terms. Rather, it was the readiness of the German masses to submit to Hitler's rule that was so profoundly disturbing. Suddenly, extreme irrationality was not expressed merely by a minority of abnormally socialized persons but apparently by an entire population of normal, well-socialized people" (Flacks, 1973, p. 55).

When reflecting on the Holocaust in 1985, even German Chancellor Helmut Kohl stated that "the decisive question is why so many people remained apathetic, did not listen and closed their eyes to the realities of an inhumane program, first discussed in the back rooms and then openly propagated in the streets" ("German Leader," 1985, p. 8). Kohl warned that the central problem should not be deciphered as the acts of a few deranged leaders.

Positive Functions of Authority

Organizations also have many positive effects on society, and they rely on the coordinated, cooperative activity of people at all levels to accomplish their ends. Saying that we should mistrust, challenge, or resist authority is hardly an answer. This would serve to undermine important and valuable functions that we depend on in organizations. Well-founded authority performs an important service in social systems:

- It serves as a focus of leadership in a crisis.
- It serves to crystallize the sense of the community when it is too large for face-to-face interaction.
- It can maintain a sense of the big or broad picture when others are immersed in particulars.
- It channels information.
- It reconciles internal interests with external demands.
- It is responsible for mentoring and subordinate development.

In the absence of an authority function, social systems can easily disintegrate.

If we needed examples of the consequences of the absence of credible centralized authority, we can look to the republics of the former Soviet Union—or even the U.S. Congress. When there is no one, no leadership, no central adhering principle, no set of ideas, no mission, then social and organizational systems at best face paralysis and gridlock; at worst, dissolution and warfare. Warren Bennis (1976b) referred to it as a sort of balkanization in our organizations, where the "politics of multiple advocacies" leads to fragmentation and the end of consensus, which is agreement reached in spite of differences.

The antiauthority tenor of many of the changes under way in our organizations should be of concern to us all. As we complain about the dearth of high-caliber leaders, it should also be noted that we are (regrettably) no longer the followers that we once were. Also lacking is the willingness to support leadership's initiatives even on a temporary basis. We claim we have reason to mistrust but little is ever going to be accomplished when the next campaign begins as soon as the just-elected take office. Neither obedience nor revolt is viable as habitual approaches to these problems. Followers and subordinates have an important role in creating (and undermining) their own authorities.

The Future of Authority

There are some efforts under way to flatten organizations through the use of more flexible organic forms and autonomous work teams. In the main, I think these efforts are positive. It is clear that steep, hierarchical, authority-driven forms are not very adaptive to changing circumstances. But such changes are not likely to occur overnight, and there is likely to be a continuing role for hierarchy and authority well into the future. While we may correctly pursue flatter or less steep organizations, some form of hierarchy (and with it, authority) is likely to be around for some time. In most organizations, such new forms will be a valuable complement to traditional hierarchy and authority, but will not do away with them.

In large-scale organizations, information processing is a core function. Economics requires some centralization of information (through specialization). It is not realistic to aspire to everyone having all information. And skill and ability will always be unevenly distributed. Further, critical contingencies will always be in flux for organizations.

As organizations move into a more on-line and dynamic relationship with their environments, different capacities will be more or less important as they are called forth to deal with changing circumstances. Those who have the critical skills and information ought to be provided authority in order to direct action and deal with changing external circumstances.

These three things alone (central information nodes, unequal ability, and shifting critical contingencies) will probably require the continuing use of some authority. People with more information, higher levels of critical skills, and access to the bigger picture *should* be granted authority in order to direct or have a larger say in systems' decisions and actions. In this, I do not advocate continuing use of rigid, fixed, and formal authority structures. I hope that the location of authority, its movement as circumstances shift, and the breadth of its prerogatives will all be more conditional and contingent in the future than they have in the past.

People *should*, under many circumstances, accommodate authority. But this should not be a habit. People in organizations should at all times maintain an on-line sense of their personal responsibility. They should be actively engaged and aware of their relationship to the whole and their contributions to often-distant outcomes. They should understand themselves in their authority relationships and know when and how to defer to authority and when and how not to. They should maintain an alertness to the values, the integrity, and the personal idiosyncrasies and flaws of those in authority. To the discerning eye, much is revealed in everyday behavior. And they should develop and maintain a strategic literacy about their organization's relation to its environment. This includes understanding its overall goals and mission, their function's goals and mission, and their alignment (with their bosses) to those larger purposes. I believe these behavioral competencies can help produce more effective, adaptable, ethical, and humane organizations.

My intention was to produce a work that could help develop those competencies.

Framing a New Theory

First, I wanted to understand how people saw their responsibilities and behavior in their relationships to people in authority. And I wanted to understand it more from a subordinate's view. How did those in these relationships see themselves, their dilemmas in relating to authority, their choices, and their decision rules for selecting among those choices?

Of course, I had known about the classical Freudian ideas (and labels) of dependence, counterdependence, and so on. But as I noticed that mental health professionals (and others) often apply these labels with abandon, very few people in organizational life see *themselves* in those terms. This left me with the question of how did and do people in subordinate roles perceive their responsibilities, and their relationship, to those in positions of authority? When they pushed back against authority or attempted to undermine it, how did they explain to themselves the reasons for their actions or values? What did they see as their range of discretion? What decision rules, if any, did they use in deciding whether to go along with, or resist, or blow the whistle on authority? What did it look like through their eyes?

Modern organizational participation creates countless opportunities, on a daily basis, to act on such values and decision rules. My method in approaching this work was designed to gain access to individual managers' thought processes and behavioral guidelines in managing themselves in their everyday relationship to organizational authority.

Aspirations in Theory Development

There were a number of aspirations that I had in the development of this theory and the creation of a research-participant learning process. I set out to pursue it in a way that allowed, encouraged, and supported learning, not just for me but for everyone. The aspiration to facilitate learning led to the identification of a number of characteristics for a new theory of authority relationships. The aspirations related to both researcher concerns as well as "user" or participant concerns.

Of course, for a researcher, it is important that any proposed theory should have elements that hang together well and relate well to other established theories and management practices. It is important that a model lend itself to identification of behaviors that can be identified by both the researcher and the participant-learner. This is to allow for both comparative analysis and for learner experimentation and observation. It should implicate both parties to the relationship.

While the focus is on the subordinate, relevant behavior is that which transpires between the boss and subordinate, not between the subordinate and his or her history. It was also important that both the process and the outcomes of the research should be organizationally based and organizationally relevant. The setting from which the data is collected, and the reference point, is the organization, and the conclusions drawn from the data are directly applicable to organizational life.

As for participant-oriented concerns, the research should be conducted in a way that does not exploit participants and itself models a good and effective authority relationship. The process and outcomes of the research should also be regarded as useful to individuals and to people in any kind of organization. If this was to be the case, the concepts needed to stay close to people's experience and be accessible to them upon reflection. A new model should employ dimensions that are recognizable to the average person (not obscured by professional terminology), and it should respect the internal logic of subordinates' world view. They should be able to see themselves in its results.

Also important in achieving this end is that the ideas are not normatively loaded, preoccupied with pathology and with conceptions about health and sickness. It seemed clear that people would shrink back from models that threatened to diagnose them into some category of illness. While the theory needed to address dysfunctionality, it should operate from a contingency view and not diagnose people into some sort of pathology. Rather it should see a wide range of behavior as acceptable and useful in some circumstances, for certain ends. The normative message to subordinates at all levels involved promoting a situational sensitivity (What is happening here?), prescriptive guidance (What approach should I use?), and adaptive competence (Changing behavior according to individual decision rules).

B. Research Methodology

Clayton Alderfer, in his article "Accepting the Discipline While Resisting the Compulsive Control of Method" (1991), refers to combining methods in behavioral science investigation. This combining, referred to as *triangulation*, brings together both field and laboratory approaches, both qualitative and quantitative methods to attempt greater understanding of phenomena under study. While he cautions researchers about its use, the concept of triangulation, of using multiple research vectors, comes close to describing the approach taken in this research. The method was iterative with both qualitative and quantitative methods and results mutually informing one another and building toward the stated results.

This research had two major phases. One I will describe as a theory-creation process, the second as a theory application and testing process.

Theory Creation

While this presentation may seem somewhat linear, the act of creating the theory was messy business. There were a lot of frustrating days, dead ends, and circular, circuitous, and tortured paths. I allowed myself certain creative inferences but then subjected them, wherever possible, to empirical testing. How well I did my job will have to await the verdict of professionals and lay users of these ideas.

Multiple Card Sorting

Initially, open-ended sentence stems were used. Approximately 150 people were asked to respond to about twenty sentence stems that began "People in authority are . . . ," "People in authority should . . . ," "When I am in contact with people in authority, I often . . . ," "When dealing with authority, I should . . . ," and so on. This group included some students, virtually all of them M.B.A.'s, and included a number of executives (from the Executive M.B.A. program at the University of New Hampshire). It also included a sample of professionals from a mental health center, a number of professional colleagues, and a group from a business client of mine.

Their responses were grouped by stems on five-by-eight-inch cards, one response per card. I then asked a number of colleagues, research assistants, and students to sort the cards in any way that made sense to them. Afterward, we discussed the sorting (which I also did), the criteria people used for their sorts, and the categories that emerged for them. Through this activity, I began to see certain dimensions of thought and behavior that seemed to guide respondents' answers and organize other raters' themes. My intention was less to develop a consensus or agreement among raters about what was there than it was to use other people's thought processes as a prompt to my own. As my ideas were forming, I often sought feedback from collaborators on whether those ideas made sense to them as well.

Interviews and Literature Search

In addition to (and concurrent with) the card-sorting process, I conducted in-depth interviews with approximately twenty mental health and behavioral sciences professionals, including social workers, psychologists, psychiatrists, and organization development practitioners.

Stir into this mixture numerous conversations with academic colleagues, students, and clients, as well as a prolonged bath in all the relevant academic and nonacademic literature I could locate.

Out of this process emerged three dimensions of variability that seemed to capture the data I had seen: the dimensions of deference, distance, and divergence. Though I had traveled my own path to these outcomes, my choices seemed to reiterate and reinforce concepts and ideas that, for the most part, were individually already circulating. Thus, I did not newly create these dimensions, although the particular coloration of each as well as their combination into the three elements of style was mine.

I had seen deference in other people's work. Geert Hofstede (1991a, [1980] 1991b) had, of course, made it (as power distance) a central issue in his cross-cultural studies. Also, Eric Berne's (1964, 1966, 1972) concepts in transactional analysis and relationship asymmetry referred to this issue as a core idea. The qualitative data from the card-sorting process and interviews also clearly revealed a concern on the part of people in subordinate roles with holding onto or letting go of power.

The concept of personal distance appeared in one work that I know of: Neilsen and Gypen's article "The Subordinate's Predicaments" (1979). They mention the dilemma of relating personally or relating impersonally to authority. My qualitative data also suggested to me that this was a core question in managers' approach to their relationships with people in authority. I could see that for some participants, people in authority were not so much people as abstractions or roles. Others seemed quite concerned with humanizing authority. I decided to elevate it to one of three core issues, versus its status as one of eight that Neilsen and Gypen proposed.

The third dimension, divergence, was not one that I recall seeing elsewhere. I later came across some work by Tjosvold on the similar notion of alignment (1990). Neilsen and Gypen (1979) did refer to a dilemma of alliance versus competition dilemma and a dilemma of mutual concern versus self-interest. These probably had an effect on my thinking, and the divergence scale (as I operationalized it) certainly does reflect elements of these ideas. Sometimes it is hard to know what came from where.

In effect, as I settled on deference, distance, and divergence, I was saying that if I knew how participants scored on each of these three dimensions, I could, with some accuracy, distinguish a style and predict their behavior in the relationship with authority.

To further test this notion, I developed a questionnaire with about sixty items that I suspected (and hoped) would tap into one or another of these dimensions. After collecting about two hundred responses to this inventory (most were from clients and Executive M.B.A. students), I conducted a factor analysis. This analysis yielded three clear factors and resulted in the questionnaire being reduced to its current length of twenty-nine items.

For the retained items, I developed an item scoring method that in most cases went from +3 to -3. When the 1 to 7 scales were transformed, each item would then load onto its scale (deference, distance, or divergence) and when combined with other items would yield a scale score. These scale scores ranged from +24 to -24 for divergence; +27 to -27 for distance; and +30 to -30 for divergence.

Theory Application and Testing

The next phase was a more convergent phase and involved obtaining a large sample for further testing of the theory and the instrument.

When I began this research process, I did so with two central concerns, in addition to that of obtaining reliable information. First, I wanted to develop a theory, a way of thinking about the issue of people's relations to authority, that would facilitate learning by people in organizations. While some attempts had been made to investigate this issue, they were relatively few and leaned in their conclusions to deep psychoanalytic views of the individual or broad-brush sociological explanations. I felt neither of these explanations explained the experience of choice (or lack of it) felt by average people in organizations. Further, neither seemed particularly useful for the average organizational participant learning about himself or herself in the relationship with authority.

Second, the research process itself could not model, as in the case of Milgram at Yale, a negative relationship to authority. For both ethical and practical reasons, the research process had to model for participants a nonabusive, nonexploitive, and empowering approach to authority in the researcher-participant relation. The challenge to me would be to handle my own authority in a way that I could hold up as responsible and effective in terms of my ends and my organization's ends, that is, research and education. At the same time, it should be ethical, empowering to others, and promoting their learning.

The ethical issue, I would think, is obvious. University professors and researchers are held in high social regard, generally trusted and deferred to. This trust required that I risk no harm of any kind to participants, particularly in risking or promoting uncontrolled (by the individual) exposure, uncritical acceptance of results, or leakage of their data.

The practical concern involves obtaining unbiased data. As the researcher-participant relationship is an authority relationship, it is likely to interact with the object of inquiry—how people react in an authority relationship. If the research relationship or the response environment itself evoked game-playing (or other) reactions from people (a common response to authority), I would end up with less valid and generalizable information. I would get less about people in relation to authority and more about their specific reaction to me or to having research carried out on them in ways they resented. I needed to manage myself and the exchange in a way that would support, not obstruct, the generation of valid data.

To satisfy both of these ends in this phase of the research, I pursued a co-inquiry research model. The objective here was to establish a partnership with participants and help them develop an investment of their own in generating valid data. To do this, I felt getting immediate feedback that they could use on their style would be giving value (participant learning) for value received (researcher learning). They would participate not just for me, but for themselves as well. To this end, I devised a scoring system that would allow participants, on completing the research inventory, to score it and get immediate feedback on their style.

In my normal work as a consultant and professor, I have a lot of opportunities to train managers and executives. I conduct sessions covering most aspects of management practice. I made learning about authority relationships (managing the relationship with the boss) a part of this repertoire. Whether I was in a university classroom or in a client system, I presented the case for the importance of learning about this relationship in much the same way as we learn about leadership styles, conflict styles, or influence styles.

Of course, some colleagues might comment that the structure of the professor-student relationship is itself coercive and eliminates choice. For the most part, I agree. But it leads us to the question of what are the legitimate functions, prerogatives, and responsibilities of people in positions of authority, in this case a professor?

My response is to note that in designing a course for students, I consider it my responsibility as an "authority" to provide learning experiences for students that will prepare them for effective participation in organizational systems. In order to do this, I continually make decisions about what they should be exposed to and what is a lower priority or even unnecessary. I take the position that understanding themselves in this key relationship is important and I unambivalently promote their learning about it. Whether their learning is then used in a research process is a different matter; it is a choice for the student that needs to be carefully guarded and preserved.

In these data collection and learning modules, I asked people to respond to the twenty-nine-item inventory (using mostly seven-point Likert scales). This takes about ten minutes. After participants completed rating the items, I briefly explained the three factors of deference, distance, and divergence. Participants then scored their own inventories using the self-scoring grid. This yielded feedback to participants on their style in managing the relationship with their boss. They obtained scores on each of the three dimensions of deference, distance, and divergence. The participants could compare their scores to the larger sample of managers or to the range of possible scores. A user manual, which was kept by the participant, explained the strengths and potential liabilities of both high and low scores on each scale as well as advice about how to complement existing skills.

At this point, I felt that they had done what I as a teacher-consultant could appropriately require them to do. They had engaged in a module designed to help them learn about themselves in authority relationships. In these learning sessions, I stressed the point that these data were the property of the participants, not the researcher. The next step had to carefully awaken them to their choices about participation in the research.

For the research agenda, participants were then asked if they were willing to have their data included in the research. If so, they were to return their inventories (the first part of the user manual) to me, along with an indication of consent for their data to be included and of whether they would be willing to participate in an interview. If willing to be interviewed, participants were asked for their names and contact information. If not, no identifiers were requested.

Anyone indicating "no" to either question on the inventory was not asked, required, or pressured to offer any explanation at all. In most circumstances, it was even impossible to identify who they were. No feedback on rate of participation was given to any client grouping. Any inventory indicating its owner did not wish to have his or her data included was promptly (and visibly) destroyed.

In the managerial sample of 630 (drawn from a wide variety of organizational settings), 382 participants (60 percent) indicated a willingness or a wish to be interviewed, and 248 participants (40 percent) indicated "no" to the interview but were agreeable to the inclusion of their data in the research base. No records were kept on the destroyed inventories but in an average group of 40 to 50 participants, there were usually 2 to 5 participants who asked that their data not be used in any way. The number was quite small and suggests no concern about nonresponse bias.

The total participant population eventually reached about eleven hundred, but (for most analyses) was reduced by eliminating undergraduate students and those indicating no organizational affiliation or background.[1] Scoring norms for the final version of the inventory were based on the 630 practicing managers and executives (401 men, 208 women, 29 indicating no gender), virtually all American. Their mean age was 39. They were overwhelmingly Caucasian (95 percent) and highly educated (14 percent had less than a bachelor's degree, 44 percent had a bachelor's degree, and 40 percent had advanced degrees). The largest sample came from business (55 percent), with smaller samples from education (15 percent), the military (7 percent), and roughly 5 percent from most other categories (health care, social services, mental health, consulting, and government).

In terms of organizational level, 8 percent of the managers identified themselves in supervision (first-level management), 35 percent in middle management, 23 percent in upper management, and 19 percent in staff positions. Worth noting is that the level bears no systematic relation to the strength of their identity as a subordinate. Sometimes higher-level managers have a stronger sense of involvement as a subordinate than they do as a manager. It appears that relatively little about this aspect of identity changes as managers move up the hierarchy. While divergence showed a relationship to level (higher-level managers were less divergent), neither deference nor distance revealed any systematic relationship to level.

Cluster analysis (K means) was performed with the executive and managerial sample using the deference, distance, and divergence variables. Various numbers of clusters were considered, but since I had theoretically derived ten clusters, I chose to ask for ten. I had noticed, for example, in my work with military officers that their patterns tended to be consistent and reflected well-known aspects of the military culture. Their responses were high on deference, high on distance, and low on divergence. While variations existed, this seemed a logical type. A rebel characterization also emerged this way as did a helper's profile. In the last, human resource professionals seemed to score more or less consistently. After a number of contacts with human resource managers, I asked them if this profile fit. Through this process, I eventually accumulated ten common clusterings.

The computer analysis yielded nine viable clusters, with one being too small ($n = 2$) for analysis. It was dropped from further analysis. Another cluster ($n = 17$) was also small but large enough and distinctive enough to be retained. The cluster analysis supported five of the ten I had theoretically constructed (Military, Helper, Rebel, Independent, and Whistleblower). It provided variations on two more (substantially what I had predicted but the scale scores were not as extreme as I had expected; Counselor, Gamesman), and revealed two that I had not anticipated at all (Diplomat, Partisan). Figure A.1 displays a three-dimensional plotting of the percentiles of the nine types on the three characteristics.

C. Assessment Inventory Statistics

The final version of the authority relations inventory was made up of twenty-seven content questions and two others that went into a relationship quality (RELQUAL) index. Eight items loaded onto the deference scale, nine on the distance scale, and ten on the divergence scale. Most questions were seven-point Likert scales. Prior to completing the inventory, all participants were instructed in the following way.

Figure A.1. Plot of the Nine Profiles.

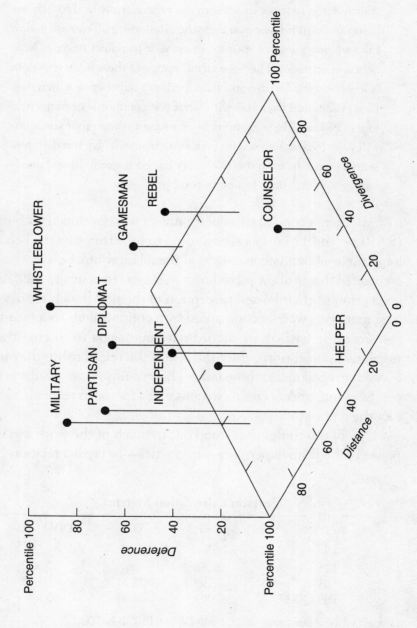

The following statements are designed to help *you* better understand your relation to those in authority in organizations and to help *me* better understand how you view the relationship. They ask you to take a "long view" of your experience or to reflect on your *basic* beliefs or attitudes. The "in general" nature of these items therefore is less concerned with a specific superior or experience which may be an exception than it is with what you commonly or frequently find to be true. There are no right or wrong answers. Your selections will yield feedback to you on your particular style. Each style represented by results from this inventory has both strengths and disadvantages. Please be as honest as you can.

Another version of this questionnaire was developed for bosses (SARO-Other) to respond according to how they saw the behavior of their subordinate managers in the relationship. Boss managers completed this to allow subordinate managers to compare their self-perception to their bosses' perception of them. All such ratings by boss managers were accompanied by a commitment to a face-to-face meeting with their subordinate managers to discuss their respective perceptions, their tasks, and the relationship they had evolved to accomplish those tasks. The inventories are available for purchase and, under certain circumstances, for use in research. Contact the author for details.

One of the things that stood out in much of the work was the power of the third dimension—divergence—to predict relationship

Pearson Correlation Matrix.

	DEF	DIS	DIV
DEF	*		
DIS	0.286	*	
DIV	-0.199	0.123	*
RELQUAL*	-0.068	0.086	0.405

Bartlett Chi-Square Statistic: 201.848 DF = 6 PROB = 0.000

Matrix of Probabilities.

	DEF	DIS	DIV
DEF	*		
DIS	0.000	*	
DIV	0.000	0.003	*
RELQUAL	0.097	0.037	0.000

Number of Observations: 591

quality (in the eyes of the subordinate managers). Goal and method alignment (or lack of it) often figured prominently in the way both boss and subordinate experienced their relationship. It suggests a much more careful attention, particularly in these times of downsizings, autonomous teams, empowerment efforts, and so on, to communicating goals and dealing with disagreements and conflicts over goals and the methods used to achieve them.

Distribution of Scale Scores

Ninety percent of the participants rated themselves at the zero point or below on the deference scale (low deference); 70 percent at the zero point or below on the distance scale (low distance); and 80 percent at the zero point or below on the divergence scale (convergent, high trust); bear in mind that the sample was overwhelmingly American. Participants obtained feedback not only on whether they were on the high or low side of the scale but on what percentile they placed in compared to other participants. The main implication of this distinction is that, on the deference scale, for example, one could score -4 and be low in the terms of the scale range. But also, as a result, this individual would score higher than 70 percent of the population on deference.

The self-report aspect of this work should be noted. Important next steps in this work will be to conduct (in addition to self-assessment) more "other" assessments and organizational climate studies (as well as obtaining samples from other cultures). I did not push this agenda as hard as I might have since there always seemed to be plenty to do in dealing with the managers' self-perceptions and learning.

Information about authority relations styles can be powerful feedback, and the climate and structure for learning in the organization must be carefully established. In the few instances where I pursued this learning with managers in client organizations, and we took care to establish that climate, the results were very positive for everyone.

Responses of assessed managers and their bosses (wherever available) supported the *general* validity of the assessments. The general concurrence in views is helpful but does not replace systematic investigation of the behavioral expressions of style.

In discriminant analysis (to be described shortly), the items from all three dimensions that predict good or bad relationships predicted many more bad relationships than the managers themselves did. This was confirmed (anecdotally) in my contacts with the boss managers too. It suggests that many subordinate managers are inaccurately assessing the relationship quality with their bosses (or at least seeing it differently than their bosses do) and the error they typically make is to assess them as better than they are (see Table A.1). This is further testimony to the need for feedback in the relationship, clearer agreement on performance criteria, and the probability that many managers' expectations regarding sponsorship and support from their bosses need to be adjusted.

Of the nine style clusters, this overestimation error was particularly pronounced in the Rebel, Diplomat, Whistleblower, and Gamesman styles. They, in particular, do not seem well attuned to the relationship costs of their styles. Such disappointed expectations can have a large consequence for individuals and organizations in determining who is selected for dismissal in corporate restructurings and downsizings. Surprising news at that time about how they are really seen (as well as a newly revealed history of distorted or missing feedback) could be contributing to the rash of lawsuits over wrongful dismissal.

Table A.1. Relationship Quality for the Nine Styles.

	Good Relationship	Troubled Relationship	Approach
Military	76%	24%	
Helper	88%	12%	
* Diplomat	74%	26%	Accommodating
Partisan	80%	20%	
Independent	66%	34%	
Counselor	82%	18%	Autonomous
* Gamesman	12%	88%	
* Rebel	41%	59%	Adversarial
* Whistleblower	40%	60%	

*Prone to overestimate relationship quality.

Factor Structure

Responses to the twenty-nine items were factor analyzed using principal components analysis with a varimax rotation. Recall that earlier factor analysis had reduced a sixty-item questionnaire to the current twenty-nine items. The analysis extracted three factors with loadings that supported the expectations. The exception is the item "exchge" (item 17), which, after rotation, loads more heavily onto the divergence scale than it does the distance scale. Because of thematic content, it was temporarily retained in the distance scale. But it would appear that the item taps into questions of vulnerability and trust and pertains less to personal distance. The asterisks indicate the items that make up the scale in the questionnaire.

Scale Reliability

The alpha for the deference scale is .547, the distance scale is .708, and the divergence scale is .773. The "X" in front of the variable names below indicates they are transformed, or recoded variables.

Factor Analysis (Rotated Loadings).

	Factor 1, DIV	Factor 2, DIS	Factor 3, DEF
SEEDIF	0.72*	-0.10	0.12
PORINF	0.68*	0.01	0.09
NOCNCRN	0.63*	0.04	0.00
SLFPRO	0.62*	0.14	0.07
DISAGR	0.58*	-0.13	0.25
ALLY	0.58*	0.20	-0.09
GOALS	0.54*	-0.15	0.12
RELATIO	0.04	0.76*	0.08
IMPERS	0.02	0.65*	-0.19
RELATI	0.20	0.63*	-0.06
CONLIM	0.19	0.62*	-0.15
ALOOF	0.05	0.56*	0.14
INTERA	0.10	0.51*	-0.18
EQUALS	-0.01	-0.05	0.60*
DEFER	0.04	0.03	0.50*
MEANIN	0.02	0.05	0.46*
EXPERT	0.34	-0.03	0.45*
RECEPT	0.10	-0.18	0.44*
INPUT	-0.04	-0.07	0.42*
LISTEN	0.44*	-0.04	0.38
EXCHGE	0.35	0.10*	-0.37
CONSULT	0.21	-0.08	0.37*
SYMBOL	0.12	0.18	0.36*
PHYSCO	0.04	0.37*	0.22
CHARIS	-0.08	0.33*	0.11
PERSON	0.12	0.43*	0.09
WATCH	0.50*	-0.01	-0.08
COMPET	0.32*	0.09	-0.03

Variance Explained by Rotated Components

1	2	3
3.70	2.99	2.24

Percent of Total Variance Explained

1	2	3
13.21	10.68	8.02

Scales were sometimes reversed to avoid habitual responses and more automatic socially desirable responses. The recoding transformation ensured consistent scale directionality.

I have been somewhat concerned about the deference scale, which is, strangely, the one concept most accepted and discussed in the literature; most of the items appear straightforward. There are some new items for this scale in testing but as yet none appears to strengthen reliability.

As I have continued in my learning about these issues, I am coming to the belief that deference has a more complex makeup than I originally thought to be the case. I am coming to see it as made up of four parts that may very well be relatively independent of one another.

One part is recognition on the part of subordinate managers about their own expertise, the feeling they have something to contribute. Such expertise may constitute a platform for influence attempts. A second belief system concerns the acceptance of personal responsibility, the belief that it is my duty to push my input. A third part concerns subordinate views toward the boss-subordinate relationship structure. This considers whether the relationship is, fundamentally, one between equals or unequals. And a fourth part concerns the belief that bosses are obligated (or not obligated) to establish structures and processes that create opportunities for input. This poses the question of whether, in the eyes of the subordinate, bosses are obligated to be receptive.

This view of the elements leaves open the possibility that a subordinate manager may believe strongly that managers should have influence with their bosses in decision making but it is up to the boss to provide the structure. Other managers who share the basic belief may see it as a matter of personal responsibility regardless of the structures provided.

Test-retest reliability with a group of approximately thirty-five M.B.A. students averaged approximately .84. Test-retest reliability study and how to distinguish random variation (noise) from

Item Reliability Statistics.

Item	Label	Mean	Standard Deviation	Item-Total R	Reliability Index	Excluding This Item R	Alpha
Deference:							
1	XSYMBOL	-0.744	1.570	.446	.700	.208	.530
2	XDEFER	-0.707	1.479	.487	.720	.272	.509
3	XCONSULT	-1.503	1.506	.501	.755	.285	.505
4	XEQUALS	-0.799	1.689	.580	.979	.351	.479
5	XEXPERT	-0.311	1.817	.514	.934	.247	.519
6	XRECEPT	-1.421	1.187	.434	.515	.259	.517
7	XMEANIN	-0.853	1.598	.504	.805	.273	.509
8	XINPUT	-0.814	1.662	.452	.751	.200	.535
Distance:							
1	XIMPERS	-1.035	1.488	.655	.974	.517	.659
2	XINTERA	0.328	1.623	.572	.928	.398	.681
3	XPERSON	-1.231	1.462	.467	.682	.294	.698
4	XRELATI	-0.624	1.654	.648	1.072	.489	.662
5	XRELATIO	0.479	1.239	.677	.838	.571	.656
6	XCHARIS	-0.073	1.228	.321	.394	.164	.715
7	XALOOF	-0.745	0.842	.452	.380	.356	.693
8	XEXCHGE	-1.151	1.471	.365	.537	.179	.718
9	XCONLIM	-1.233	1.441	.633	.911	.495	.664
10	XPHYSCO	1.752	1.663	.480	.799	.283	.703
Divergence:							
1	XWATCH	-0.609	1.647	.526	.866	.371	.763
2	XCOMPET	-1.137	1.643	.414	.680	.243	.780
3	XALLY	-1.478	1.598	.568	.907	.426	.756
4	XDISAGR	-0.011	1.547	.599	.926	.468	.750
5	XGOALS	-0.779	1.578	.558	.881	.416	.757
6	XLISTEN	0.321	1.335	.481	.642	.352	.764
7	XSEEDIF	-0.630	1.491	.700	1.044	.597	.733
8	XNOCNCRN	-1.170	1.524	.628	.956	.505	.745
9	XSLFPRO	-0.175	1.693	.629	1.066	.491	.747
10	XPORINF	-1.280	1.341	.658	.883	.558	.741

accurate assessment of changed phenomena posed both practical and ethical problems. Presumably the individual learns on completion of the inventory the first time. Retest should (unless first-time results are withheld and the individual knows nothing of the factors) show differences. Such differences would not mean the inventory is unreliable but that the phenomena itself has changed. For the investigator, to withhold information for a considerable period of time seems questionable in both moral and practical terms; to provide such information results in confounding outcomes. Use of comparator groups would perhaps provide an answer but is extremely difficult to execute with its own significant flaws.

D. Additional Findings of the Research

Subordinate Identity of Managers

In an earlier phase of this research, I set out to discover how managers thought of themselves in terms of their identity as managers of others versus their identity as subordinates.

To pursue this issue further, I asked managers about this dual identity, the idea of being a manager and a subordinate at the same time. My interest was to discover how practicing managers, some at high organizational levels, thought about themselves in their roles as managers.

I assumed that both conceptions or images of themselves were required. They needed to think about self-as-manager *and* self-as-subordinate, inasmuch as both described their work reality. I asked fifty-four managers to allocate 100 points between the two following descriptions according to how they saw themselves at work. The descriptions I gave them were these:

A. I am someone who has authority and managerial or supervisory responsibility. I am someone who makes decisions, gives guidance and direction, allocates resources, and takes responsibility for my subordinate's work and development.

B. I am someone who has a reporting relationship "upward" to someone else. In this sense, I am a subordinate who receives direction and guidance; someone who strives to obtain and maintain influence with my superior(s), tries to understand my superior and copes with feelings of vulnerability.

The following responses are a sample of the results.

	A(Manager)	B(Sub.)
District Manager, Corp. Planning	40	60
IE Manager, HQ Large Multinational	60	40
USAF Wing Commander	80	20
Executive Director, YMCA	30	70
Manufacturing Manager	80	20
Production Supervisor	50	50
Refinery Manager	70	30
Marketing Manager	60	40
Manager, Corp. Attorney	10	90
State Veterinarian	10	90
Technical Services Manager	40	60

This data set is intended to be illustrative, but it (and the larger data set) confirms several points about this issue of managerial identity.

1. Subordinate identity (overall) is a strong, on average almost equal, portion of self-concept. Averaging these identity weights for these fifty-four managers, who are in most cases managers of considerable elevation, reveals the average distribution of 56 percent for their managerial identity and 44 percent for the subordinate identity.

Issues about being an effective subordinate are important to managers, even upper-level managers. Executives often complain to me that no one ever talks to them in development or training sessions about this issue.

2. Sense-of-self as a subordinate bears no clear relation to organizational elevation. In the survey managers were asked to assign themselves to one of five organizational levels, from first-level supervision to top-level executive. Statistically, there is no significant correlation of managerial identity weightings with organizational level. Classical wisdom or intuition would lead us to expect that as people progress higher up the hierarchy, their sense of themselves as subordinates would give way to their sense of themselves as managers. This is not so. This aspect of identity is not, to any significant degree, dependent on elevation.

Other research data support this. When sorted by level, there are only rare differences in authority relationships that occur as a result of movement up the hierarchy. In my research data, the only thing that seemed to clearly change as managers moved up was they tended to see things differently than their bosses less frequently (less disagreement on goals, methods, procedures) and they tended to see their bosses less as a competitor for recognition and promotion. Interestingly, this shift did not extend to seeing their bosses more as allies *or* feeling less need to be self-protective around their bosses. So, to these people, at all levels, it makes as much sense to talk to them as subordinate managers as it does to talk to them as leader managers.

3. This identity changes quite a bit. It is fluid. Depending on the task or the job they are doing, who their boss is, their frequency of contact with their boss, and other elements of the relation, executives point out that these are changeable identities. The Air Force wing commander commented to me that he feels quite "managerial" until his commanding general shows up on his horizon (which he does frequently). Then his identity "does a full 180-degree shift." Others also spoke of the changeability of this identity from day to day and week to week. It depended a lot on what activity they were engaged in. All agreed that they needed to shift frequently and that it is a complex activity for subordinates to manage their shifting

conceptions of themselves, their various role relationships, and the operating contexts they worked in.

Myers-Briggs Type Indicator

I conducted a small study involving fifty undergraduate organizational behavior students. At different times in their semester the class completed both the authority relations inventory and the Myers-Briggs Type Indicator (Briggs and Myers, 1985). Item and scale correlations were done, with some interesting (but I would say only suggestive) results.

In the case of the extraversion-introversion scale, extraversion is associated with lower deference, lower distance, and higher divergence (the Rebel style, which is in fact characterized by a more outgoing orientation to authority relationships). Introversion shows no significant relationships with deference, distance, or divergence.

Sensing is positively and significantly correlated with a role orientation with people in authority (high distance). Sensers are described as practical, realistic, matter-of-fact, not given to ferreting out the patterns that underlie concrete experience. They are dependent on authority for sense making and tend to defer as they maintain something of a personal distance.

There is a strong link between intuition and low deference. As opposed to its scale partner "sensing," which is an appreciative, fact-gathering orientation, intuition "shows meanings and relationships and possibilities that are beyond the reach of your senses" (Briggs and Myers, 1985). It is "especially useful for seeing what you might do about a situation" and is a more normative or prescriptive orientation. It would make sense that individuals so oriented would lean toward pushing their point of view in relationships with people in authority. Intuition is also strongly connected with low distance or a more personal orientation to relationships with authority.

Thinking orientations are connected to higher distance or role orientations in the relationship with authority and are strongly connected to a high-divergence or low-trust orientation with people in authority. The thinking orientation is described as "impersonally . . . predicting the logical result of any particular action" (Briggs and Myers, 1985). The thinking orientation is associated with the more technical disciplines and refers to a preference for dealing with the "part of the world which behaves logically (like machinery) with no unpredictable human reactions." It is probable that such an orientation, when viewing the complex political calculations and multiple agendas that upper management authority must serve, would find such a decision-making process unscientific and illogical.

A strong connection occurs between the feeling orientation and low distance in the relationship with authority. This is not surprising, since the feeling orientation places more value on people's feeling and subjective, interpersonal relations.

On the judging-perceiving scale, judging appears to be weakly associated with higher divergence or low trust for authority. As described, those with a judging orientation prefer to live "in a planned, decided, orderly way, wanting to regulate life and control it" (Briggs and Myers, 1985).

While going through all the styles and associations would be prohibitive and not particularly revealing as there are many equivocal associations, it is interesting to see the convergence of descriptions based on the above findings with a particularly common Myers-Briggs profile, the ESTJ.

According to the Myers-Briggs Type Indicator, the description of this type includes the following phrases: practical realists, matter of fact; natural head for business or mechanics; not interested in subjects they have no use for, but can apply themselves when necessary; preference for impersonal analysis; effective at finding flaws; like to organize and run activities; tend to run things well especially if they remember to consider other people's feelings and points of view when making their decisions; stand firm against opposition.

This correlational study suggests this person would be oriented to low deference (pushes for influence with authority), high distance (establishes more of a role orientation), and high divergence (goal incompatibility, low trust). Such a profile (L,H,H) corresponds to the Gamesman style, described earlier.

The description of this person's authority relationship orientation included such phrases as: well-educated technical people, often (when in business) in R&D; commonly report being in virtually constant struggle with the organizational hierarchy and the authority structure; resigned acceptance of relationship inequality and status differences but also a strong need to have influence; operates in a detached manner, maintaining high personal distance; the reticent technical; people in authority are not allies or are even competitors; bosses have little concern for the subordinate's interests and needs and the subordinate needs to be self-protective at all times. Gamesmen are resistant to the boss's directions and tend to reject them (often covertly) as ill considered.

Discriminant Analysis

Discriminant analysis suggests items that predict membership in one or another of two groups. It reveals eight items that discriminate between those who report good relationships with authority and those that report bad relationships with authority. They are listed below with the scale on which they load.

#4	Intera; Distance
#8	Compet; Divergence
#14	Equals; Deference
#15	Expert; Deference
#16	Goals; Divergence
#17	Exchg; Distance
#19	Meanin; Deference
#24	Nocncrn; Divergence

I interpret these indicators to mean that a troubled relationship with people in authority is created by a belief system characterized by the following behavioral elements. First, resist inequality in the relationship and refuse to accept the idea that power in organizations is distributed unequally (a democratic ethos). Along with this, maintain a strong sense of yourself as an expert and resist moving into the implementer role in order to make your boss's directives happen.

Second, maintain a lot of personal distance with your boss and keep your interactions objective without revealing any doubts, questions, or insecurities. Maintain a sort of wall. Let the boss see your discomfort with any kind of personal exchange.

Third, carry a low-trust orientation into the relationship with differing (but unarticulated) views of goals. A necessary corollary to this view is the belief that you are in competition with your bosses for recognition and promotion and that your bosses are generally not concerned with your well-being.

There is an interesting example of these differences and how the three dimensions interact in the contrast between the Counselor (VL,VL,M) style and the Rebel (L,L,H) style. In a number of ways similar on the ratings, the Counselors report 18 percent of their relationships with people in authority as troubled while the Rebels report 59 percent as troubled (and this is probably an underestimate). Yet the Counselors push their bosses much more strongly for influence than do the Rebels. There is no significant difference on education.

It appears that there are much different relationship consequences when managers establish a fuller personal connection with their bosses, as the Counselors do. It is likely that the higher divergence rating of the Rebels creates more of an adversarial cast to the relationship but their strategic approach to self-disclosure appears to substantially worsen the quality of their relationship to their bosses.

African-American Managers

Though the sample of African-American managers is small ($n = 17$), t-test analysis comparing group means indicates some significant differences and confirms what other research has found and many would intuitively suggest.

There are no overall differences between African-American and Caucasian managers in the sample on items such as education, level, and overall assessments of relationship quality with their bosses. However, race does seem to make a significant difference in a number of subscales. In general, African-American managers differ from their white counterparts in their orientation to establish much more role-oriented relationships with their bosses. This is not unexpected, as many have observed the cultural insensitivity and white male bias in most organizations. The role orientation is a protective device in an environment where revealing the self can be viewed as politically unwise. Results on divergence also indicate a much stronger need felt by African-American managers to protect themselves in their relationships with people in authority.

There are a few items in the deference scale where this group scores differently than the Caucasian majority. This refers to substantially less willingness on the part of African-American managers to defer to their bosses and less acceptance of boss-subordinate inequality. The numbers are too small to offer any certain conclusions, but it would appear that these managers are more likely to appear in the autonomous and adversarial styles than they are in the accommodating styles.

These managers' self-assessments of relationship quality may be in error; they may be overestimating the quality of their relationships with their bosses. The overall style orientation (of lower deference, higher distance, and higher divergence) suggests a leaning to the Gamesman style, one that is noted for its poor relationship quality. Yet the statistics on the self-report of relationship quality show no differences here. Perhaps the answer is in recognizing that discriminant analysis shows predictions of many more bad relationships than are reported. This was particularly true for the autonomous and adversarial styles, the Gamesman among them.

African-American managers, it would appear, tend toward an understandable but problematic way of relating to their bosses. And, it would further appear that they, like many of their Caucasian counterparts, are unaware of the probable relationship costs and effects on their careers, effectiveness, and so on.

Loevinger's Ego Development Scale

A sample of ninety managers completed the authority relations inventory and were assessed on Jane Loevinger's scale for ego development. It was found that those at higher levels of ego development tended to be substantially lower on the deference scale. This greater inner direction makes sense as higher ego levels are typically associated with a stronger internal sense of one's own authority and heeding one's own internal voices.

Also, higher ego development was strongly associated with lower personal distance in authority relationships. Those at higher levels of development tended toward greater personal involvement and interactions with authority. This suggests a tendency not to view authority as a remote object but rather as an organizational role occupied by similar (to the self) and fallible humans. Identification rather than objectification is the orientation.

On the divergence scale, averages for those at higher ego levels were not significantly different than scores for those at lower ego levels. What was different was the amount of variance for high versus low ego level managers. There was much greater variation for those at high levels than there was for those at lower levels. It suggests that higher ego levels are associated with more contingent (and hence variable) behavior. This is also an expected outcome for high-stage awareness.

Such a combination of low deference, low distance, and variable divergence comes closest to the Counselor profile (it is in the forty-ninth percentile on divergence). This is a group that, in spite of its aggressive nondeference and significant divergence, reports very high relationship quality with authority. It is the *only* low-deference group that reports high relationship quality.

Notes

Chapter One

1. I first saw this story related in Charles Perrow's book *Normal Accidents: Living with High-Risk Technologies* (1984).

Chapter Two

1. He did, however, get some exposure to the impact of national culture on a visit to the United States in 1909. Sadly, after his visit Freud became one of America's most vehement critics. Among other things, he noted the very weak rule of official authority and what he considered to be the exaggerated elevation of the average person. He argued that the absence of and refusal to accept authority led to "superficial understanding, inconstancy of allegiance and incessant bickering" (Kaye, 1993, p. 122). He left deeply disappointed.

2. My research found that high-deference managers tend to report smoother, more harmonious and less troubled relationships with their bosses than do low-deference managers. They report the relationships as more comfortable but not more effective. This is in a way understandable, but it is also unfortunate; pushing for influence with the boss, while probably useful much of the time for effectiveness, appears to have some relationship risks.

3. McClellan's lack of deference for (particularly) Lincoln's authority was legendary. McClellan once returned from an

evening out to be informed that the president was waiting for him in his parlor. He sent an aide downstairs to tell Lincoln that the general was tired, had gone to bed, and could not be disturbed. For his part, Lincoln commented that he would willingly hold the general's horse if he would bring the president victories.

Chapter Four

1. Gender differences stand out here. Men, in their twenties, peak on divergence and over time become more convergent, never again attaining the level of their early years. Women start off as significantly less divergent than men, but around age thirty start a curve upward that continues into the middle to late forties. This echoes the concerns of those who have encountered the glass ceiling as we see women become more divergent in their approach to authority.

2. These data suggest that, if relationship placidity and agreeableness, not necessarily effectiveness, are prime values, the best subordinate strategy involves high deference, low distance, and low divergence: the Military profile.

Chapter Five

1. During the statistical analysis of this group, which my computer had labeled cluster 7, I began to have flashbacks to a type of organizational participant described by Michael Maccoby in *The Gamesman* (1978). As I reviewed his description of his Gamesman manager, my cluster 7 subordinate appeared quite similar. Hence the label stuck.

Chapter Six

1. The recipe for very poor relationships is low deference, high distance, and high divergence—the Gamesman style.

2. One of the interesting findings of my research is that boss managers tend to rate their subordinate managers as more deferential (higher on deference) than subordinate managers rate themselves. When a subordinate manager thinks he or she is pushing, most boss managers see a lot of tentativeness. The implication is that, in most cases, subordinate managers have more room to push than they take advantage of.

Chapter Eight

1. I sometimes wonder whether the wish to have no authority reflects more of our change agents' personal attitudes than it does organizational needs. While often portrayed as a harsh, arbitrary, confining element, authority plays an important, useful, and beneficial role in organizational life. Some of those who occupy the role do it badly, but let us be careful not to throw the baby out with the bath water.
2. The population of educational administrators and managers in this research is for the most part drawn from university settings. It remains to be seen whether these observations on culture would characterize other educational systems as well.
3. Father Mulcahy was closest to their image of the ideal subordinate, Hawkeye Pierce the furthest from that image.
4. The ideas here about ethics and dialogue are largely derived from Srivastva and Associates (1988), especially Chapter Twelve.
5. In this, I have found Nancy Adler's book *The International Dimensions of Organizational Behavior* (1991) useful and informative.

Appendixes

1. It is worth noting that undergraduates tend to fall into the Whistleblower cluster, showing high deference, high distance, and high divergence.

References

Adler, N. *The International Dimensions of Organizational Behavior*. Boston: PWS/Kent, 1991.

Alderfer, C. "Accepting the Discipline While Resisting the Compulsive Control of Method." *Journal of Applied Behavioral Science*, 1991, 27(3), 265–268.

Arendt, H. *Eichmann in Jerusalem: A Report on the Banality of Evil*. New York: Viking Penguin, 1963.

Baird, L., and Kram, K. E. "Career Dynamics: Managing the Superior-Subordinate Relationship." *Organizational Dynamics*, Spring 1983, pp. 46–64.

Beachy, D. "Bad Bosses a Common Cause of Worker Stress, Survey Says." *Houston Chronicle*, Oct. 14, 1992, p. 1.

Beer, M., Eisenstat, R. A, and Spector, B. "Why Change Programs Don't Produce Change." *Harvard Business Review*, Nov.-Dec. 1990, pp. 156–166.

Bennis, W. "Leadership: A Beleaguered Species?" *Organizational Dynamics*, Summer 1976a, p. 5.

Bennis, W. *The Unconscious Conspiracy: Why Leaders Can't Lead*. New York: AMACOM, 1976b.

Benson, D. J., and Thompson, G. E. "Sexual Harassment on a University Campus: The Confluence of Authority Relations, Sexual Interest and Gender Stratification." *Social Problems*, Feb. 1983.

Berger, P. L., and Luckmann, T. *The Social Construction of Reality*. New York: Doubleday, 1967.

Berkley, G. *How to Manage Your Boss*. Englewood Cliffs, N.J.: Prentice Hall, 1985.

Berlew, D., and Harrison, R. "Topic Introduction on Power and Influence." In D. A. Kolb, I. Rubin, and J. Osland (eds.), *Organizational Behavior: An Experiential Approach*. Englewood Cliffs, N.J.: Prentice Hall, 1991.

Bernardin, H. J. "Subordinate Appraisal: A Valuable Source of Information About Managers." *Human Resource Management*, Fall 1986, 25(3), 421–440.

Berne, E. *Games People Play: The Psychology of Human Relationships*. New York: Grove Press, 1964.

Berne, E. *Principles of Group Treatment*. New York: Oxford University Press, 1966.

Berne, E. *What Do You Say After You Say Hello? The Psychology of Human Destiny*. New York: Grove Press, 1972.

Block, P. *The Empowered Manager: Positive Political Skills at Work*. San Francisco: Jossey-Bass, 1987.

Bolman, L. G., and Deal, T. E. *Modern Approaches to Understanding and Managing Organizations*. San Francisco: Jossey-Bass, 1984.

Bowen, C. D. *Miracle at Philadelphia: The Story of the Constitutional Convention, May to September, 1787*. Boston: Little, Brown, 1986.

Boyatsis, R. E. "The Need for Close Relationships and the Manager's Job." In D. A. Kolb, I. Rubin, and J. Osland (eds.), *Organizational Behavior: An Experiential Approach*. Englewood Cliffs, N.J.: Prentice Hall, 1991.

Boyatsis, R. E., and Skelly, F. R. "The Impact of Changing Values on Organizational Life." In D. A. Kolb, I. Rubin, and J. Osland (eds.), *Organizational Behavior: An Experiential Approach*. Englewood Cliffs, N.J.: Prentice Hall, 1991.

Briggs, K. C., and Myers, I. B. *Myers-Briggs Type Indicator*. Palo Alto, Calif.: Consulting Psychologists Press, 1985.

Brown, L. D. *Managing Conflict at Organizational Interfaces*. Reading, Mass.: Addison-Wesley, 1983.

Cates, R. S. "The Trojan Horse: How Bad Ideas Infiltrate Good Companies." *Management Review*, July 1991, pp. 22–24.

Cohen, A. R., and Bradford, D. L. "Influence Without Authority: The Use of Alliances, Reciprocity, and Exchange to Accomplish Work." *Organizational Dynamics*, Winter 1989, pp. 4–17.

Cohen, A. R., Fink, S. L., Gadon, H., and Willits, R. D. *Effective Behavior in Organizations*. Homewood, Ill.: Irwin, 1988.

Crary, M. "Managing Attraction and Intimacy at Work." *Organizational Dynamics*, Spring 1987, pp. 26–41.

Crockett, W. J. "Dynamic Subordinacy." *Training and Development Journal*, 1981, *35*(5), 155–164.

Culbert, S. A., and McDonough, J. J. "The Invisible War: Pursuing Self-Interest at Work." In P. Frost, V. Mitchell, and W. Nord, *Organizational Reality: Reports from the Firing Line*. 3rd ed. Glenview, Ill.: Scott, Foresman, 1986.

Daft, R. L. *Organization Theory and Design*. St. Paul, Minn.: West, 1989.

Deal, T. E., and Kennedy, A. A. *Corporate Cultures: The Rites and Rituals of Corporate Life*. Reading, Mass.: Addison-Wesley, 1982.

Diamond, M. A., and Allcorn, S. "Psychological Barriers to Personal Responsibility." *Organizational Dynamics*, Spring 1984, pp. 66–77.

Drucker, P. F. *The Practice of Management*. New York: American Management Association, 1954.

Dyer, W. G., and Dyer, J. H. "The M*A*S*H Generation: Implications for Future Organizational Values." *Organizational Dynamics*, Summer 1984, pp. 66–79.

Feynman, R. P. *"What Do You Care What Other People Think?"* New York: W. W. Norton, 1988.

Flacks, R. *Conformity, Resistance, and Self-Determination.* Boston: Little, Brown, 1973.

Gabarro, J. J. "When a New Manager Takes Charge." *Harvard Business Review*, May-June 1985, pp. 110–123.

Gabarro, J. J., and Kotter, J. P. "Managing Your Boss." *Harvard Business Review*, Jan.-Feb. 1980, pp. 92–100.

Garsombke, D. J. "Organizational Culture Dons the Mantle of Militarism." *Organizational Dynamics*, Summer 1988, pp. 46–56.

"German Leader Decries Holocaust." *Boston Globe*, Apr. 22, 1985, pp. 1, 8.

Gilley, J. W., and Moore, H. L. "Managers as Career Enhancers." *Personnel Administrator*, Mar. 1986, pp. 51–59.

Greenberger, R. S., and Langley, M. "Intrepid Marine." *Wall Street Journal*, Dec. 31, 1986, p. 1.

Halberstam, D. *The Reckoning.* New York: Morrow, 1986.

Hall, J. "Communication Revisited." *California Management Review*, 1973, *15*(3), 56–67.

Hebden, J. E. "Adopting an Organization's Culture: The Socialization of Graduate Trainees." *Organizational Dynamics*, Summer 1986, 46–65.

Heller, T. "Changing Authority Patterns: A Cultural Perspective." *Academy of Management Review*, 1984, *10*(3), 488–495.

Hofstede, G. *Cultures and Organizations: Software of the Mind.* New York: McGraw-Hill, 1991a.

Hofstede, G. "Motivation, Leadership, and Organization: Do American Theories Apply Abroad?" In D. A. Kolb, I. Rubin, and J. Osland (eds.), *The Organizational Behavior Reader.* 5th ed. Englewood Cliffs, N.J.: Prentice Hall, 1991b. (Originally published in 1980.)

Holusha, J. "A Call for Kinder Managers at G.E." *New York Times*, Mar. 4, 1992, p. D1.

Janis, I. *Victims of Groupthink.* Boston: Houghton Mifflin, 1972.

Kaye, H. L. "Why Freud Hated America." *Wilson Quarterly*, Spring 1993, pp. 118–125.

Kegan, R. *The Evolving Self: Problem and Process in Human Development.* Cambridge, Mass.: Harvard University Press, 1982.

Kelley, R. E. "In Praise of Followers." *Harvard Business Review*, Nov.-Dec. 1988, pp. 142–148.

Kelley, R. E. *The Power of Followership.* New York: Doubleday/Currency, 1992.

Kelman, H. C., and Hamilton, V. L. *Crimes of Obedience: Toward a Social*

Psychology of Authority and Responsibility. New Haven, Conn.: Yale University Press, 1989.

Kerwin, K., Treece, J. B., and Schiller, Z. "GM Is Meaner but Hardly Leaner." *Business Week*, Oct. 19, 1992, pp. 30–31.

Kets de Vries, M.F.R., and Miller, D. *The Neurotic Organization: Diagnosing and Changing Counterproductive Styles of Management*. San Francisco: Jossey-Bass, 1984.

Kiechel, W., III. "When Management Regresses: Hard Times Are Sending Some Bosses Back to the Stone Age." *Fortune*, Mar. 9, 1992, pp. 153 ff.

Klein, M. *Envy and Gratitude & Other Works, 1946–1963*. New York: Dell, 1975.

Kotter, J. P. *The General Manager*. New York: Free Press, 1982.

Kovach, B. E. "The Derailment of Fast-Track Managers." *Organizational Dynamics*, Fall 1986, pp. 41–48.

Krantz, J. "The Managerial Couple: Superior-Subordinate Relationships as a Unit of Analysis." *Human Resource Management*, 1989, 28(2), 161–176.

Livingston, J. S. "Pygmalion in Management." *Harvard Business Review*, Sept.-Oct. 1988, pp. 121–130.

Lombardo, M. M., and Eichinger, R. W. "Rescuing Derailed Executives." *Issues and Observations*, Fall 1988, pp. 1–5.

Longenecker, C. O., and Gioia, D. A. "SMR Forum: Ten Myths of Managing Managers." *Sloan Management Review*, Fall 1991, pp. 81–90.

Lorsch, J. W., and Mathias, P. F. "When Professionals Have to Manage." *Harvard Business Review*, July-Aug. 1987, pp. 78–83.

McCall, M. W., and Kaplan, R. E. *Whatever It Takes: Decision Makers at Work*. Englewood Cliffs, N.J.: Prentice Hall, 1985.

McClelland, D., and Burnham, D. "Good Guys Make Bum Bosses." In D. A. Kolb, I. Rubin, and J. Osland (eds.), *The Organizational Behavior Reader*. 5th ed. Englewood Cliffs, N.J.: Prentice Hall, 1991. (Originally published in 1975.)

Maccoby, M. *The Gamesman*. New York: Bantam Books, 1978.

Mainero, L. A., and Tromley, C. L. *Developing Managerial Skills in Organizational Behavior*. Englewood Cliffs, N.J.: Prentice Hall, 1989.

Mapp, A. J., Jr. *Thomas Jefferson: A Strange Case of Mistaken Identity*. Lanham, Md.: Madison Books, 1987.

Mechanic, D. "Sources of Power of Lower Participants in Complex Organizations." *Administrative Science Quarterly*, 1962, 7, 349–364.

Milgram, S. *Obedience to Authority*. New York: HarperCollins, 1974.

Mills, E. W. "Cult Extremism: The Reduction of Normative Dissonance." In K. Levi (ed.), *Violence and Religious Commitment: Implications of Jim Jones's People's Temple Movement*. University Park: Pennsylvania State University Press, 1982.

Mintzberg, H. *Power in and Around Organizations*. Englewood Cliffs, N.J.: Prentice Hall, 1983.

Moore, B., Jr. *Injustice: The Social Bases of Obedience and Revolt*. Armonk, N.Y.: Sharpe, 1978.

Morgan, G. *Images of Organization*. Newbury Park, Calif.: Sage, 1986.

Morris, R. B. (ed.). *The United States Department of Labor History of the American Worker*. Washington, D.C.: U.S. Government Printing Office, 1976.

Muczyk, J. P., and Reimann, B. C. "The Case for Directive Leadership." *Academy of Management Executive*, 1987, *1*(3), 301–311.

"Munitions Expert Says Top Officials Knew of Contra Military Operation." *Boston Globe*, July 26, 1988, p. 5.

Neilsen, E., and Gypen, J. "The Subordinate's Predicaments." *Harvard Business Review*, Sept.-Oct. 1979, pp. 133–143.

Perrow, C. *Normal Accidents: Living with High-Risk Technologies*. New York: Basic Books, 1984.

Peters, T. J. *Thriving on Chaos: Handbook for a Management Revolution*. New York: Knopf, 1988.

Peters, T. J. *Crazy Times Call for Crazy Organizations*. New York: Vintage, 1994.

Peters, T. J., and Waterman, R. H. *In Search of Excellence: Lessons from America's Best-Run Companies*. New York: HarperCollins, 1982.

Presthus, R. "Patterns of Organizational Accommodation: Upward-Mobiles, Indifferents, and Ambivalents." In J. Shafritz and P. Whitbeck (eds.), *Classics of Organization Theory*. Oak Park, Ill.: Moore, 1978.

Rediker, M. "Life Under the Jolly Roger." *Wilson Quarterly*, Summer 1988, pp. 154–166.

Reiterman, T. *Raven: The Untold Story of Rev. Jim Jones and His People*. New York: Dutton, 1982.

Reutter, M. "The Rise and Decline of Big Steel." *Wilson Quarterly*, Fall 1988, pp. 47–85.

Rhodes, L. "That's Easy for You to Say." In R. L. Daft and M. P. Sharfman (eds.), *Organization Theory and Cases*. 3rd ed. Minneapolis: West, 1990.

Schama, S. *Citizens: A Chronicle of the French Revolution*. New York: Random House, 1990.

Schein, E. H. "Organizational Socialization and the Profession of Management." In D. A. Kolb, I. Rubin, and J. McIntyre (eds.), *Organizational Psychology: Readings on Human Behavior in Organizations*. Englewood Cliffs, N.J.: Prentice Hall, 1984.

Schlesinger, L. A., and Oshry, B. "Quality of Work Life and the Manager: Muddle in the Middle." *Organizational Dynamics*, Summer 1984, pp. 4–19.

Schumacher, E. F. *Small Is Beautiful: Economics As If People Mattered*. New York: HarperCollins, 1975.

Simon, Y. R. *A General Theory of Authority*. Westport, Conn.: Greenwood Press, 1962.

Smircich, L., and Morgan, G. "Leadership: The Management of Meaning." In D. A. Kolb, I. Rubin, and J. Osland (eds.), *The Organizational Behavior Reader*. 5th ed. Englewood Cliffs, N.J.: Prentice Hall, 1991. (Originally published in 1982.)

Srivastva, S., and Associates. *Executive Integrity: The Search for High Human Values in Organizational Life*. San Francisco: Jossey-Bass, 1988.

Tannenbaum, R., and Schmidt, W. "How to Choose a Leadership Pattern." *Harvard Business Review*, May-June 1973, pp. 162–175.

Tjosvold, D. "Flight Crew Collaboration to Manage Safety Risks." *Group and Organization Studies*, 1990, *15*(2), 77–101.

Turner, V. *The Ritual Process: Structure and Anti-Structure*. Ithaca, N.Y.: Cornell University Press, 1977.

Tusa, A., and Tusa, J. *The Nuremberg Trial*. New York: Atheneum, 1984.

Vaill, P. B. *Managing as a Performing Art: New Ideas for a World of Chaotic Change*. San Francisco: Jossey-Bass, 1989.

Veiga, J. F. "Face Your Problem Subordinates Now!" *Academy of Management Executive*, 1988, *2*(2), 145–152.

Weber, M. *The Theory of Social and Economic Organizations*. A. M. Henderson and T. Parsons, trans. New York: Free Press, 1947.

Weick, K. *The Social Psychology of Organizing*. Reading, Mass.: Addison-Wesley, 1979.

Wills, G. *Inventing America: Jefferson's Declaration of Independence*. New York: Random House, 1978.

Wolfe, D. M., and Kolb, D. A. "Career Development, Personal Growth, and Experiential Learning." In D. A. Kolb, I. Rubin, and J. Osland (eds.), *The Organizational Behavior Reader*. 5th ed. Englewood Cliffs, N.J.: Prentice Hall, 1991.

Yukl, G. A. *Leadership in Organizations*. Englewood Cliffs, N.J.: Prentice Hall, 1989.

Zaleznik, A. "The Dynamics of Subordinacy." *Harvard Business Review*, May-June 1965, pp. 119–131.

Zaleznik, A. "Managers and Leaders: Are They Different?" *Harvard Business Review*, Mar.-Apr. 1992, pp. 126–135.

Zimbardo, P. G. "A Pirandellian Prison: The Mind Is a Formidable Jailer." *New York Times Magazine*, Apr. 8, 1973, pp. 38 ff.

Index